So you are thinking of moving to France

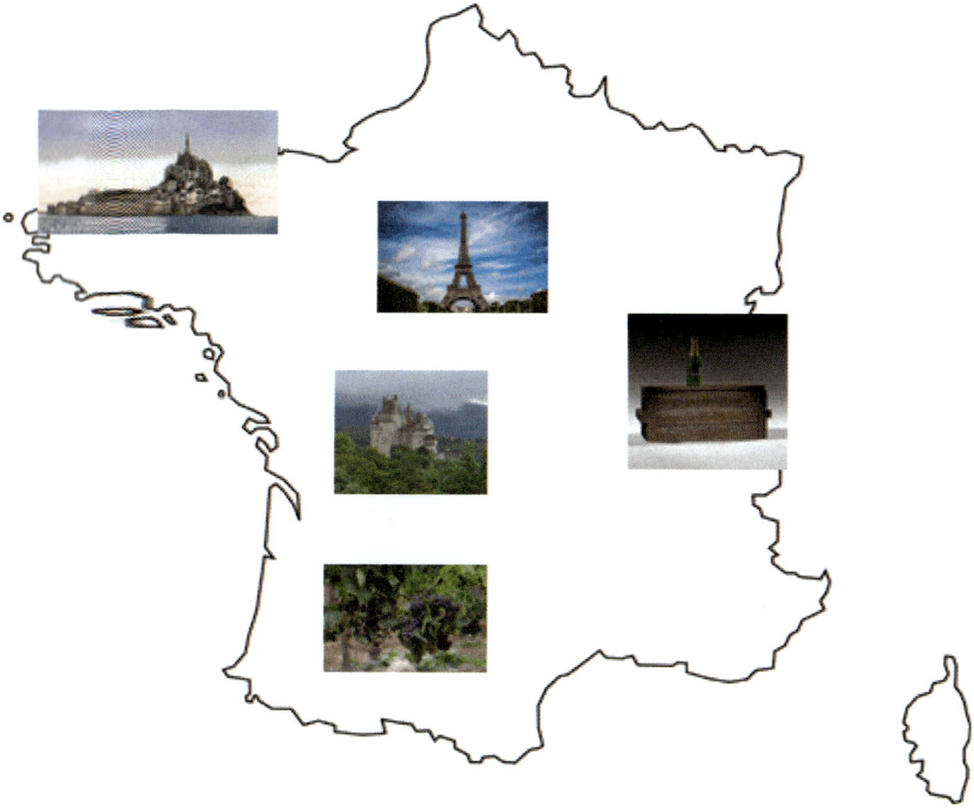

A practical guide, hints and tips from someone who did just that

David Sontag

First published June 2019

© David Sontag 2019

errors and omissions excepted

All rights reserved
Without limiting the rights under copyright
reserved above, no part of this publication may be
reproduced, stored in or introduced into a retrieval system,
Or transmitted, in any form or by any means (electronic,
mechanical, photocopying, recording or otherwise), without the
prior written permission of the copyright owner

Independently Published

ISBN-13   978-1-0736-3553-5

So You're Thinking of Moving to France

 Beware coming out without a clear focus, just because you have fallen for France isn't enough, otherwise you will find yourselves pulled from pillar to post looking at all manner of properties without having a clear idea of what you want or what will work for you. Especially if you just book a couple of days out with a single agent and ask them to show you what they have in their portfolio (that meets your basic criteria).

It is easy to get seduced by the size of properties. The typical grounds on offer with rural properties here by far and away exceed what you might expect for your budget in the UK and it is easy to underestimate what you are potentially buying. If you are sports minded then you can easily get an idea of comparable sizes; Wembley as marked out for soccer is around 0.72 ha (1.8 acres) whereas Twickenham with its larger pitch and dead ball areas extends to 0.88 ha (2.18 acres). Do not take on more than you can comfortably manage. You want to be a Human Being not a Human Doing so you do not want to spend all your time working or paying someone to do it for you, you want to be able to get out and enjoy your new environment, after all that is why you want to move here, right?

2.2.3 Research in Depth

There are plenty of avenues to follow that will assist in your research depending on how much time you have available (we had more than most as our UK Property Sale fell though twice thus extending the time we had before we moved out). For example:

a. Holiday to/visit different parts of the country to aid your decision;
b. Attend Property Shows, not so much to look for properties themselves but for all the other exhibitors that attend, Banks, Currency Exchange Companies, Estate Agents, Language Learning, Multi-lingual Solicitors, Removal Companies, Tourist Boards etc. and also to sample the various regional food delicacies;
c. Look online for the above types of enterprise
d. Make contact with them & try and understand the business rules and regulations etc. that apply to any business you propose establishing;
e. Subscribe to relevant magazines; and
f. Subscribe to relevant newsletters, estate agent or otherwise.

So You're Thinking of Moving to France

outcome had been decided knowing full well that the house we had chosen met our 'Why' irrespective if what was supposed to happen and also ticked almost all our other boxes.

Of course then soon after the other advantages of French country living; vis: less people, open spaces, outdoor living, relaxed lifestyle, slower pace and better quality of life became added bonuses.

 Don't forget to remove the rose-tinted spectacles from time to time though. Have no illusions, moving to modern day rural France is like stepping back in time to an England of 40-50 years ago; but some of the more modern aspects of life like banking, e-commerce etc are somewhat dated at times and it is easy to get frustrated with the slow pace. If you are retired however just take it in your stride, there is always tomorrow.

2.2 Decide your strategy

Are you an impulsive or pre-meditated type? By that I mean are you the sort that once you have the idea you just want to get on with it or are you more considered, more measured, and take your time to research and plan out your moves?

2.2.1 How are you going to sell your UK Property?

By this I mean think long and hard about whether you want to embark on a complex overall transaction that ties a UK based sale in with a French based purchase or whether you want to or are able to stage them. For a start you are dealing with two different legal systems and the fact that by comparison the English system is back loaded, i.e. exchange of contracts generally happens a few months into the purchase whereas the French system is front loaded with the *Compromis du Vente* coming soon after the cooling off period. There is also the question of cost, phasing everything to tie in is clearly quite complicated, you will need bi-lingual UK Solicitors and you will pay out more in fees to enable it to happen.

2.2.2 How to find your French Property

Are you happy uncovering properties and finding out information about them on the internet or are you a more touchy feely sort of person wanting to examine them close up in the first instance?

So You're Thinking of Moving to France

2. Finding "the One"

2.1 Establish your Why?

The reasons behind our move were quite simple, to enjoy more spacious surroundings, the slower pace and quality of life and to be able to live mortgage free. I said earlier that we felt it was right place right time for us as our various children had all left home and were confidently living their own lives and so we decided that after years of thinking about them and putting them first that it was time we did something for us.

At the time I was worried I might be bored when we got here so our initial criteria for buying a house included properties that were either large enough to section off or had their own *Gites* I could run.

It is important to establish your Why?
- Are you simply retiring?
- Do you need to keep a house back in the UK?
- Do you want to live full-time in what was your Holiday Home?
- Do you want bilingual children or to be bilingual yourself?
- Do you want to buy somewhere to move in/renovate?
- Do you want land/a small-holding or more space than you have?
- Do you need somewhere that provides a form of income?
- If so how often do you want/need to work?
- If so how much do you need?
- Do you intend relocating here but working back in the UK?

All of these factors will influence both the type of property that you need and its location, use these to drive your search. Simply finding a house, falling in love with it and moving in is a potential recipe for disaster. All dreams need to be underpinned with some kind of foundation else they will quickly turn into a living nightmare.

Once you have found your 'why' it will motivate you through the difficult times ahead of actually moving in and help you ignore outside influences or 'noises off' that can distract and dissuade you.

We saw our house and signed the *Compromis du Vente* before the 'referendum on the EU' in June 2016, we then moved in after the

So You're Thinking of Moving to France

were both our own boss, and we knew we could take early retirement if we wanted to. Above all we figured that it was now 'time for us' and although we might be 7-800 miles away from the bulk of the family modern technology meant that we could make a telephone or video-call with ease and because of low cost air-travel the children and their families could come and visit us whenever they wanted to and enjoy true quality time in a relaxing environment.

More importantly we also didn't want to look back in say 10 years' time, think of what might have been and have regrets that we never grasped the opportunity to move when we could. We very much wanted to live the dream and as you only get one life we decided to live it?

1.2 The Layout

After this background section I have laid out this guide as follows:
- Section 2 discusses finding the 'One';
- In Section 3 I talk about how to prepare for your move; and
- Section 4 concentrates on the move itself;
- In Section 5 I cover the settling in period;
- Section 6 moves on to address the practicalities of daily living;
- In Section 7 there is a short discussion of the type of tools that may become everyday essentials; and
- Section 8 looks at those devices that you might wish to use inside the home to simplify life there.

Where I think you would benefit from avoiding the specific traps that we fell into I use this warning symbol.

Where I think there is something not generally known I show it using this symbol

Any specific tips or suggestions for you the reader are indicated by these symbols

So You're Thinking of Moving to France

1. Background

1.1 The Trigger

Why did we want to move to France? To a degree it was 'right place right time' syndrome. My wife had spent a number of happy holidays here when she was younger and also when she first had her children. I on the other hand had experienced a couple of enjoyable 'drive through France with the lads' type holidays but really fell in love with the country when I was lucky enough to work in Paris for eight months. It was during the year of the Bicentenary, and also the Centenary of the Opening of the Eiffel Tower, and I was assigned to a British Bank in *Place Vendôme*. It was convenient for me, flying out of Stansted (from what is now the Business Terminal but then the only terminal) into Charles de Gaulle on a Monday morning and returning back home on a Friday afternoon.

Shortly after starting there I moved out of the Hotel I was staying in with fellow consultants and rented a furnished apartment in Neuilly, near the business district of La Defense. From my balcony on the fourteenth floor overlooking the Seine I could see the Eiffel Tower off to the South East, and in front of me the top of the Arc de Triomphe was just visible, and off to its left in the hills of Montmartre stood the Sacre-Coeur. Life couldn't get any better. Each day I joined the commuters on the No. 1 Metro line and travelled into Tuileries station. As the months wore on I started staying at weekends particularly during the summer, so captivated was I by the scenery and way of life.

Years later, in 2012, after my stint as a Gamesmaker at the Olympics and Paralympics Joanne and I stayed in a friend's farmhouse near *Belves* in the southern *Dordogne* for a week. We absolutely loved it and it was here that our two earlier worlds collided. When we returned to the UK we found we both missed it terribly and the following month after a particularly arduous commute home I said that I wanted us to move to France. During the hold-up on the train I had figured out we could easily sell up and live mortgage and stress free, and so our journey began.

You could think us selfish but our various children had left home and although we were both working at the time we took the decision we

So You're Thinking of Moving to France

About the author

David was born and brought up in North London before moving to the somewhat greener pastures of mid-Essex in the early eighties. After leaving school he studied Computing and pursued a career in that field working as a Computer Programmer and then as a Systems Analyst, subsequently moving into Project and Programme Management and then Consultancy. After he was made redundant he setup his own Private Service Company and worked on his own account providing Programme, Project Management and Business Change Consultancy to a range of public and blue chip private sector clients for 20 years before taking early retirement. He then spent 18 months assisting a friend with her newly acquired Travel Franchise, by introducing rigour into her quoting and booking processes, improving her social media focus and increasing her followers through creation of a publicity video and weekly newsletter.

David is married to Joanne, a former gift shop proprietor who had never found a Gift Shop selling exactly what she wanted so opened her own and spent the next 20 years being the Chief Fairy in her own Curiosity Shop. They have five children between them, four grandchildren and live in a small village/commune of around 900 people in the *Corrèze*, one of 3 *départements* that comprise the *Limousin* Region, part of the new administrative area of *Nouvelle Aquitaine* (created on 1st January 2016). They live there with their two dogs: Alfie an 8 year old Border Collie, the 'Black One' who they've had since a pup, undisputed leader of the pack, a sometime neurotic, ultra protective, mummy's boy who will run all day if it means chasing sticks; and Keno (a former street dog, who they adopted /rescued 2 years ago) a 4 year old Berger Blanc Suisse, the 'White One', inquisitive, hyper alert, and 6 stone of youthful excitability, exuberance and occasionally misdirected wayward energy, he loves chasing lizards and digging holes to try and catch Mice, Moles and Mole rats.

Since moving to France they have embraced the French lifestyle and their *raison d'être* has become:

'Live the life you love and love the life you live'

So You're Thinking of Moving to France

Introduction

Why write this guide?

When my wife and I eventually moved to France from Essex back in the summer of 2016 it was the culmination of almost 4 years effort. We thought we had done a lot of research, both in terms of where we wanted to live and the process we would go through to get there. We moved into a newish house – it was only 6 years old at the time – but since then we have encountered numerous pitfalls and potential problems that had to be overcome. None were insurmountable but it has been very much a voyage of discovery since and in some instances we have found out things the hard way as 'Strangers in a Foreign Land'.

I have never published anything before but we have certainly experienced all manner of problems/situations since arriving in France, involving different interactions that required speaking at least some French that I think make me reasonably well qualified to write such a guide, for example:

- Buying a car from a garage;
- Buying various electrical appliances in store;
- Dealing with a wasp infestation in the roof;
- Understanding/getting familiar with all manner of new tools;
- Explaining to an Insurance company 'Expert' what happened after we had an [above ground] swimming pool 'burst';
- Getting quotes to replace an unsafe veranda/deck;
- Erecting almost 400yds of fencing to keep our dogs safe;
- Ejecting a three generational family from our garden after they climbed over a fence to steal chestnuts;
- Having to find an emergency dentist 2 days before Christmas;
- Ordering 27 tonnes of stones from a quarry for resurfacing and then telling them their invoice was wrong;
- Returning to find our car badly damaged while we had been having a picnic whilst watching horse-racing;
- Suffering storm damage to the house;

Table of Contents

Introduction 1
1. Background 5
2. Finding "the One" 7
3. Preparation 22
4. The Move 29
5. Settling In 33
6. Everyday Living 48
7. Boys Toys 75
8. Domestic Gadgets 88
Annex A – Questions for Estate Agents 1
Annex B – Useful Addresses 1
Annex C – Public Holidays 2019 1
Annex D – Public Holidays 2020 1

So You're Thinking of Moving to France

What it's not!

> Firstly this guide is not a discussion about the shambles of Brexit and the implications of it if you plan to move to France. In fact the word does not appear in any of the following text. If the politicians eventually make up their mind and decide what is happening I will revise appropriate sections of text as necessary once the implications become clear. Until then it is so much speculation and I won't waste any effort writing about it.

Secondly there are many comprehensive guides out there which will explain for example how best to establish one's fiscal residency or how to apply for your Carte Vitale as part of accessing the French Healthcare system once you are here. Equally there are those many publications that talk about making the most of one's retirement etc. etc. I do not intend trying to compete with these guides and so will generally leave anything that requires technical or specialised knowledge well alone. Research those things elsewhere and look in here for the practical implications of doing or using same.

Thirdly this is not a treatise on how to restore or renovate an old house. It is not something I have done and would not care to offer anyone advice about it other than use your common sense, draw up a sensible plan for so doing, don't set impossible deadlines and budget accordingly.

Finally I do not intend making lots of recommendations as to what to buy or where to buy it from, nor endorse specific products, that is not what this guide is about. Similarly I will not look to tell you where to go or what to do as there are many tourist type publications out there that are far more detailed than I could hope to be. Besides, that is outside my scope and you'll find out all that in your own good time when you are good and ready.

So You're Thinking of Moving to France

- Having to recover data from and subsequently replace a damaged hard-drive on my laptop;
- Being summoned to the Tax Office to answer queries on our tax return;
- Separately returning to the Tax Office because their system would not allow us to set up our tax account online;
- Arguing with the local *Chasse* about incursions to our garden;
- Needing to trap Coypu *Ragondin; and*
- Removing a fallen tree from our small lake *Etang.*

Consequently I thought about writing this book and also because various friends and 'friends of friends' had asked me about the different aspects of moving here so I aggregated and expanded all my advice in one place. It is the sort of guide that, had it been available at the time of our move, would have helped us enormously to prepare, settle in and to understand a range of things that are not immediately apparent until they happen to you. The guide is centred around helping someone move to a semi-rural location like us (although it can't cover every situation in every *département*) rather than being a guide to big city life but even then I hope there will be certain nuggets that you can take from it and use. It is based on our personal experiences but where relevant it also draws on some (anonymous) friends' experiences with selecting and settling into their French properties before enjoying 'La Belle Vie'.

As such I hope it is full of useful 'Hints and Tips', simple distilled common sense-statements of the blindingly obvious and practical suggestions and insights that will hopefully smooth your transition into a different culture, a bygone age almost. As it's one that people say is like how the UK used to be 40-50 years ago, with its friendliness, openness and lack of fear.

Where applicable, French words/phrases are included *In this format*. Although note that if you encounter a French word that is spelt as you would find in English, it <u>will</u> invariably be pronounced differently.

Dedication

To Joanne, for knowing that my dream was your dream and vice-versa, thank you for sharing it with me and embarking on this wonderful journey together.

Also to Josh, Ella and Lady, you would have loved it here.

Acknowledgements

Front page designed by David Sontag,
courtesy of copyright free images from   http://www.pixabay.com

Screenshot of Cadastral plan from   http://www.cadastre.gouv.fr
Screenshot of Etalab/Valuations from   https://app.dvf.etalab.gouv.fr/

Lightbulb icon from free clipart on   www.vecteezy.com
Suggestion icon from free clipart on   www.clipartpanda.com
Tip icon from free clipart on   www.clker.com
Warning icon from free clipart on   www.publicdomainvectors.org/

All other images   © David Sontag

If you have any comments/questions about the material herein then feel free to contact me on davidsontag@outlook.com

So You're Thinking of Moving to France

- Close to (walking distance) /on the edge of a town/village;

As well as ready accessibility of a:
- Bakery;
- Bank;
- Bar;
- Doctors;
- Petrol Station;
- Supermarket; and
- Vets

and relatively easy access to an Airport and a Train Station if we needed them. We were lucky in that we have all of these and as added bonuses we have 4 other Supermarkets within a 10 minute drive, a Chateau and a Racecourse nearby as well a National Stud with a multiplicity of free equestrian events throughout the year. We also have a local Rugby Club that plays to a reasonable standard (in addition to a professional team in Brive, a short drive away) which ticks my own personal box. However flexibility is keynote, as it is in many areas of life.

Define your search area – else it will limit /complicate any viewings.

2.4   Ask questions to narrow down your search

The amount of information that you get from estate agents *Immobiliers* is as varied as it is in the UK, some are better than others. The main difference is, that in the UK, unless you are relocating it is relatively easy to find the property whose details you have been sent and drive by as part of your preliminary assessment. In France it is a little trickier. There are two reasons for this, one is that the addresses are a lot vaguer in some instances. Simply naming a house in a commune doesn't give you, the house hunter, much to go on, and the second reason is that agents don't necessarily like pinpointing the property on a map as they are quite protective of their right to show you round.

Next is the habit of giving room sizes expressed in square metres. A $16m^2$ bedroom sounds attractive but this obscures say a usable 4m*4m room from one that is 8m*2m and far less practical.

So You're Thinking of Moving to France

2.2.4 Rent before buying

Once you have decided on the area you want to move to, something to consider if you are able, depending on the money you have available and the commitments you have in the UK is to find somewhere to rent in that area. Out of season you should be able to rent a holiday home or a *Gite* for a relative song compared with doing the same at the height of the summer. So doing will enable you to live and breathe as a local, to examine what facilities are available in the wider area, uncover what will be going on in July and August – many French villages come alive in the summer months with night markets, fayres etc. and become familiar with what may become your local bar, *bibliothèque*, *boulangerie* or *supermarché* and instinctively know if it's right for you.

2.3 Location, Location, Location

This adage is certainly true when you move to foreign climes. What do you want? A rural idyll, edge of civilisation or the middle of town?

By comparison to England, France is a huge country, over 4 times the size and what looks close by on a map may not be in reality. Remember that what is attractive in the height of summer might not be in the depths of winter or indeed vice versa. Staying somewhere that requires you getting in a car and taking a 15-20 minute drive to the shops may be suitable for a couple of weeks holiday but you will soon get bored with it on a full-time basis. Be aware also that outside of the big cities/towns public transport is few and far between and taxis are prohibitively expensive.

When you come from a typical housing estate in the UK the prospect of the nearest neighbour being half a mile away is extremely attractive, but what if you have an accident or need help, are just missing human contact and want to chat over the fence, or are snowed in and need some basic provisions? Will it still appeal/seem practical then?

When I talk about location I am not just talking about which area of France you want move to, I'm talking about what defines your ideal property, not just the house but the other factors that will impact your new life. For example when we were looking at properties the main box that we wanted ticking was as follows:

So You're Thinking of Moving to France

doesn't provide a definitive legal definition, although if required you can establish this through a formal land survey. If you know the basic property details then you can readily access the Cadastral plan, (See Annex B for more information).

The website is easily navigable and is available in English, French and Spanish. The initial display is a map of France, you can then zone into a specific Department if you want or enter the *lieu dit* the Commune, Town or Post Code. Your search then returns a list of upto 10 *Parcelles*. Conversely if you get sent the details from the Estate Agent you can confirm them here.

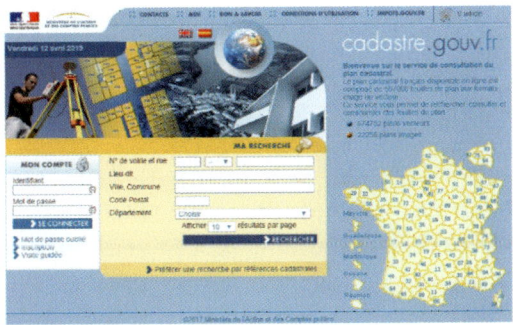

The cadastral plan and the *Parcelles* that it shows is very important because of some of the idiosyncrasies of French properties compared to those in the UK. Three examples from houses that we looked at spring to mind all of which had on the face of it had a reasonable amount (in excess of one hectare) of land attached. Consequently beware of houses:

1) With land or buildings on both sides of a road.
   Sure you can 'drive' the road using Google Maps before viewing if you are lucky but that will not necessarily show you how busy it is. If you have to keep crossing the road to get to another part of your garden or garage you need to consider how safe it might be so to do, not just for you but for your children, your animals, friends etc.
2) With land that isn't contiguous.
   You read that a property you are interested in has a certain amount of acreage with it but either when you get there or if you check it out

So You're Thinking of Moving to France

Allied to this is that a large number of older French houses have rooms leading off of rooms, particularly bedrooms. Whilst this might be acceptable if you have a young family it clearly won't work as the premise for a B&B or operating *Gites*. How do you get round this?

Well simply ask for a floorplan, we only encountered one (British Owned) agency that routinely gave floorplans as part of the details they provided. Even if they are not to scale they give you some indication of proportionality. You'll be told that they don't produce them in which case ask the agent to hand-draw one and send that across. The thought of a possible sale will motivate them.

Also ask for more photographs (than the ones necessarily on the agents website). Attractive sounding bedrooms may have chest high beams running across them – something you might tolerate for a week's holiday but not living there full-time.

During our internet based research on potential houses to ultimately go and view, we developed a list of some two dozen questions or so that we sent to agents when talking to them about one of their properties. From this we were able to discount a vast number of houses and so greatly simplify our viewing trips. See Annex A for further insight.

2.5 Cadastral Plan

In France the equivalent of the UK Land Registry is the Cadastral Plan. This was first created in the Napoleonic era to assist with calculating land tax and is now ultimately maintained by the French tax authority, the *Direction Générale des Finances Publiques (DGFiP)*. Basically all of the *Départements* are divided up into numbered plots on which ownership of the land is based and are shown graphically (although they do not provide details of the owner of a property or (necessarily) all the land parcels in a single ownership). It is helpful to home buyers because it shows individual buildings, the relative size of the plot and the place name *lieu dit*, of the property together with the specific cadastral numbers to which it belongs.

Another note of caution here, the cadastral plan does not show precise boundaries between neighbouring properties so consequently it

So You're Thinking of Moving to France

beforehand using the *Cadastre* you find that one or more *Parcelles* are actually someway distance/down the road. This may inhibit your access or equally make the property seem less attractive depending on what you are looking for.

3) With inset land that doesn't belong to you.
We looked at one property that had a one acre field separated from the bulk of the garden by a smallish copse, consequently it wasn't immediately visible from the house. In this field there was a large rectangle of land stretching inwards from the adjacent road that actually belonged to a third party. Immediately we started thinking about safety of our dog, Alfie. Would this party allow us to fence along the road and put a gate in for their access, what if they were in the habit of just turning up to mow this land and he saw/heard/smelt them? He is extremely protective and the problems it might cause didn't bear thinking about. Equally we saw another property which had a large tract of land surrounding the house and running down to a busy road actually had a small square cemetery plot within it and we were told that there were regular visitors to same.

2.6   Trying to Establish a Fair Price

From a UK house buying perspective there is a missing part of the jigsaw when it comes to buying a house in France. For almost 25 years now it has been possible for potential purchasers to access HM Land Registry 'price paid data' which contains the sale prices of all properties in England and Wales that have been submitted to HMLR for registration. This enabled one to see how values had changed over time, although obviously one couldn't see the properties actual condition. Yet in France there was no direct equivalent. Consequently one was pretty much in the dark when it came to determining property values and one paid what one could afford and/or what one thought was reasonable (compared with say something similar back in the UK).

Until recently this information could be obtained but only by paying a Notaire for information but new laws aimed at greater introducing transparency to the property market mean that one can now get relevant details of property sales in the last 5 years from a map of the

So You're Thinking of Moving to France

area in question through means of a Government site. (See Annex B for more Information)

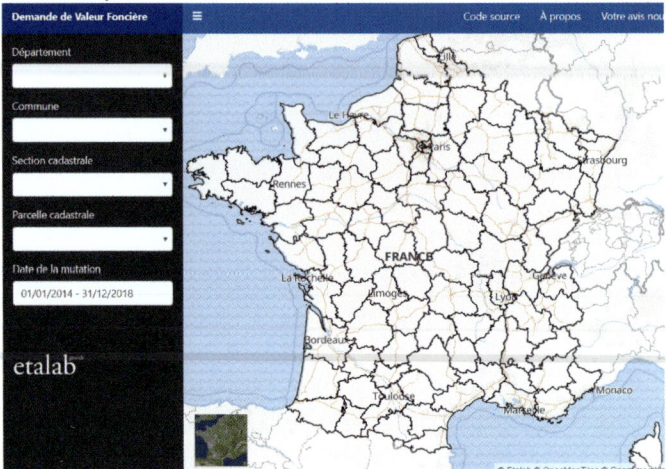

This will enable you to build up a picture of what you think the house is worth, after that it is as much a lottery as house buying is in the UK.

2.7   Your Viewing Trip(s)

Once you have a target property(s) in mind bear in mind the housing market in France is quite different to the UK, houses are sometimes on the market for many months, consequently when you ask to see somewhere you are rarely told you have to wait. Even with what are in fact holiday homes (*maisons secondaire*) there is usually a local person who has a key and looks after the place for the absent owners who could give you/agent access.

If practicable carry out a preliminary recce of areas you've seen property advertised in. In our case simply driving around from Toulouse to Bordeaux and 600 miles in between circling areas on the map that looked lovely and crossing out areas to avoid paid dividends. Unless we had done this we wouldn't have known about the Nuclear Power Station at *Golfech* (some 25km from *Agen*) as that is visible, and to our thinking, a blight on a large swathe of the adjacent countryside.

So You're Thinking of Moving to France

As I have already said France is a big country, you need to be fairly systematic when it comes to looking at property otherwise you will spend a long time in the car and be driving backwards and forwards. To this end we did not help ourselves because as a result of our recce' we expanded our search from the *Belves* area and started requesting details about houses in the *Dordogne* before including *Tarn & Garonne* and *Lot & Garonne*. You'll notice the *Corrèze* didn't feature!

With my professional background we didn't just decide to view houses because we liked reading their details, I developed a grid to effectively score the different types of house based on what was important to us (See section 2.3). We then ranked the properties according to their score. Then using their location (or at worst commune) I plotted them on a map and worked out the best route between them along with getting an idea of travel times. At that point I contacted agents and said we want to view this house on this day and ideally around this time, allowing say an hour and a half to two hours per property depending on its size. It sounds very directive but the agents fell in with this approach and very few rejected it.

When you are out and about viewing, particularly if you are driving to meet an agent, travelling to somewhere you have arranged privately, trying a drive-by or indeed you may only have been given a house name and a commune which covers a huge area. If your SatNav can't make head nor tail of the directions you have been given remember if you get to the main village in the commune go in and ask for directions at the Mairie. They will certainly know where the houses are.

Obviously another approach is simply to book a couple of days out with a single agent and spend time with them looking at all the properties they may deem suitable for you. We did this on a couple of occasions and it did introduce some potential candidates into the mix.

When assessing a property, particularly if it has a significant amount of land attached compared with what you are used to in the UK, it is easy to get carried away with the house and its grand sweeping vistas but remember you need to be able to manage the grass or pasture. What is more you will need a plan for when you are older and possibly not as

So You're Thinking of Moving to France

physically capable as you once were? A note of caution here, French Agents are aware that one of the attractions of their properties to English buyers is the comparative amount of extra space so they almost always start you outside in the garden/grounds with which you invariably think are wonderful until you go inside. It is then you may realise that you can't live with the beam across the bedroom or the staircase behind the door and wish you had gone inside first.

2.8 Perseverance is the Key

If you are lucky the house whose details you have fallen in love with will become exactly that, your dream home. If however it isn't, for any number of reasons, and none of the other properties are either, do **not** get despondent, the right one is out there, you just have to find it.

Once we had finally exchanged contracts on our English sale we made three separate viewing trips in all. One the week before we downsized in England, the second the week after and at the end of that we were quite despondent and had wondered whether we would ever find a home in France. Yet we still had two high scoring potential properties to view. One had been out of the way geographically from our second trip and the owners of the other had been on holiday and it had taken time for the agent to source a key, when they did we were a good 3 hours drive away from it so they kept it until we could return for another trip.

That third trip was 3 weeks after moving during which we drove down from Essex as opposed to hiring a car from Limoges Airport. We visited both of those houses and a few others besides and it is the trip where our perseverance bore fruit. By the end of it we had visited 48 properties in all, returning to 2 of them so had 50 total visits in 13½ days of viewing and driven a total of some 4400km. Our 'one' which provided the *Cri de Coeur* was number 47 (the 49th visit), **perseverance does pay**!

If however you find 'the One', fall in love with it and plan to open a B&B, Campsite, or business from scratch, then don't assume that you can despite what the agent says. The land may well have planning considerations attached and 'Change of Use' may either not be possible or if it is you may find there is an unexpected price-tag to go along with

So You're Thinking of Moving to France

it, so either check it out before you make a formal offer or draw up a relevant Condition Suspensive (See section 2.8.4) before embarking on the sales process. My former industry had a well used saying, 'Don't assume, it makes an Ass of U and Me'.
Don't let that apply to you!

2.9   The French Sales Process

Hopefully your viewing trip(s) bear fruit at which point you will engage with the buying process so I can't continue this section without a mention of certain parts of the French Sales process. I do not intend explaining these steps in great detail but will comment on certain aspects of it that you may not be aware of.

> **My disclaimer here is that as I am not legally qualified you should check all salient points with the relevant professional.**

2.9.1   Offer Secures

Should you be lucky enough to find 'the One' be aware that one difference with the French house buying process is that if you offer to buy at the asking price (even verbally) then providing the terms are clear, a contractual commitment arises and the Vendor is obliged to sell the property to you.

2.9.2   Cooling Off

Once the contract for the Sale and Purchase has been prepared then French law allows the buyer a ten day cooling off period in which to withdraw from the purchase for no reason without penalty.

2.9.3   Notaires

The property sale that you are progressing towards is handled by a *Notaire*. These are public officials appointed by the Minister of Justice and it is mandatory for anyone selling a house to use them. Although appointed by the state they are <u>not</u> paid by them, rather they are paid for by their clients according to a scale of charges laid down by the state for the services that they perform. Incidentally they normally charge you an over estimate of the fees involved, payable in advance, with any

So You're Thinking of Moving to France

balance being returned after the sale has completed and all the appropriate paperwork has been registered, usually some months later.

They are not the same as a Solicitor that one would use in the UK as they are concerned purely with ensuring that the process is followed correctly and consequently do not work for either the Vendor nor the Purchaser. I did not feel entirely comfortable with this approach and so appointed my own *Notaire*. In such cases it does not cost any more, the two *Notaires* simply split the statutory fee between them.

If you are lucky your Agent may recommend a *Notaire* who speaks English which clearly simplifies things but you are obviously at liberty to engage a translator and take them along to any signing (at additional cost to you of course). Equally you could employ a UK based bilingual solicitor to work on your behalf and liaise with the *Notaire*.

2.9.4 Condition Suspensives

As the Sale and Purchase agreement is being drawn up you as the buyer (and indeed the Seller) have the opportunity to include certain conditional clauses within it, these are known as *Condition Suspensives*.

For example the common types of inclusions might be that the purchase is subject to:

- you, the purchaser obtaining a mortgage for the property;
- a satisfactory outcome of a House Survey – although I suggest that this would need to be defined in greater detail as 'satisfactory' means all things to all people.
  (Note that surveys before purchase are by no means as common in France as they are in the UK);
- confirmation of a particular boundary issue;
- obtaining specific planning consent;
- the purchase (or sale) of adjoining or constituent *Parcelles* of land; or
- that the Vendor includes the land tractor/mower in the actual sale.

Basically any significant thing that you want confirming before you agree to buy the property, your agent or *Notaire* will be able to advise you on what is a suitable inclusion. If whilst looking around the property you see something that isn't mentioned in the property details and that you

So You're Thinking of Moving to France

expect to remain, i.e for you to acquire as part of the purchase, then I suggest you propose a suitable condition. We expected some 8m^3 of wood stored under our veranda to be included in our purchase; it wasn't, and we hadn't thought to make it a condition of purchase!

Where they have been included the agreement will also state the date by which a condition precedent must be fulfilled. If it is not satisfied by this date the Purchaser or Vendor can withdraw from the deal, although it will be subject to the detailed contract conditions.

As a buyer one can't use conditional clauses as a way of simply gaining more time to decide whether or not one wants to proceed with the purchase!

2.9.5 SAFAR

It was the involvement of SAFER (*Société d'aménagement foncier et d'établissement rural*) in our sale that came out of nowhere as far as we were concerned. We only became aware of their potential involvement in our purchase when we were gathered for the signing of the *Compromis du Vente*. (See section 2.8.6) SAFAR is a body you will undoubtedly encounter if you are looking to buy property in rural France. The reason being that this government agency has the right of first purchase (*droit de pre-emption*) on a great deal of rural property that comes onto the market in France.

The principle behind this is to assist young farmers and help them become established as well as to rearrange agricultural assets into more viable entities. The agency also has some rural & environmental development obligations where they might enforce their right to help local councils or other public bodies.

Notaires have an obligation to notify SAFER of all sale and purchase contracts, after which the agency has two months to decide whether it wishes to use its right of pre-emption. So although you may think you are on the threshold of moving to France when you sign the sale contract with your seller, in practice you have to wait until SAFER have had an opportunity to buy before you can start counting your chickens!

So You're Thinking of Moving to France

In practice, the vast majority of rural property transactions go through without SAFER showing any interest, although clearly those properties where such agricultural interests are obviously involved do merit close scrutiny. If they decree that they are interested it does make life difficult & can blow a hole in your plans as it can result in the Vendor withdrawing the sale or being required to sell to SAFER who have an automatic right of purchase if they accept to buy on the terms of the sale contract.

Do not despair, if time is indeed of the essence you cannot circumvent the involvement of SAFAR in your potential purchase but you can speed it up so you know the outcome much quicker. Payment of 300 € (as of 2016) will get you a result within one month rather than two and you should instruct your *Notaire* accordingly.

2.9.6   Exchange and Completion

Basically what we in the UK call Exchange of Contacts is called the *Compromis du Vente* in France and it happens towards the start of the overall process, a discrete period after the end of 'Cooling Off' rather than the end; and what we would call Completion is known as the *Acte du Vente*.

What surprised us was at different times in both the *Compromis* and *Acte* stages whilst sitting in the *Notaire's* office both Joanne and I were asked to copy out various paragraphs **in French** to include in said documents and this was completely unexpected. A somewhat strange spidery text ensued from both of us as these days most writing is done at a keyboard and other than application forms I cannot personally remember when I last had to write out anything more substantial than a couple of sentences. What is more we then had to initial the bottom corner of each page before signing at the end. All in all a far more extensive involvement in the contractual side than one would expect in the UK and in our case quite nerve wracking. Not just for the legalities of what we were getting into but knowing we had a tight timetable to meet to catch our flight home as we hadn't allowed for any of this extra time.

 If you barely write anything these days then spend a bit of time making sure that what you do write is legible so it doesn't cause problems on the day.

So You're Thinking of Moving to France

3. Preparation

So now all being well you have found 'the One' and the sale process is ticking along, on the assumption that you will be ready to move once it finishes, i.e you are not waiting for anything in the UK. What can you usefully do to simplify your transition?

3.1   Improve your language skills

I accept that people buy properties for all sorts of reasons and we have met many long-term residents who barely speak any words of French. Of course those people are happy to live in an artificial bubble, watching and reading English TV and newspapers, using mobile British Hairdressers sticking with British friends and not making the effort to speak French.

This does not sit well with me. One does not have to be fluent but I think it only right that if you freely choose to live in another country that you should be proficient in some aspects of the language, so I would implore you to spend some of the time learning/improving French. Do not become one of those 'Brits abroad' who expect everyone they meet to speak English and when questioned by a local just speak louder and in so doing give the rest of us a bad name. After all if you were still in the UK and for example some Albanians or Laotians moved in next door you wouldn't necessarily speak to them in their native language and you would expect them to know some English wouldn't you?

3.1.1   Online Resources

There are many online resources out there to choose from, pick something that works at your pace but try to devote at least 10-15 minutes each day to acquiring new words/phrases. Believe me the great feeling you get when you have just been into the garage to book a service or made a [cold] telephone call to arrange/ask something and not a word of English has passed your lips is reward itself. Even after getting on for 3 years now I still try and learn some French every day and take a weekly 1 hour lesson. Unless you are a language graduate it is unlikely to come naturally so you need to work at it every day.

So You're Thinking of Moving to France

3.1.2 Stickers

Once you know your move is happening, or even during your search If you are truly committed, put stickers/post-it notes on various items around the house with the French description for the item to get you used to thinking differently.

In the build up to the exchange of contracts on our English Sale I placed stickers all over the kitchen to familiarise ourselves with the French names for every day appliances etc. just to get us started.

3.1.3 Ban English

During the prelude to your move as well as once you are established in your new residence it is a good idea to agree to talk French for periods of time. Even with a limited knowledge of French you can both agree to say spend 10 minutes a day, why not start with breakfast, speaking basic French. If one of you has a better aptitude they can help the weaker one in a sheltered friendly environment.

3.2 Utilities

There are now well over 100 electricity suppliers in France, it is not just EDF anymore, and there are at least a dozen gas suppliers. As you might expect there is competition for Internet, Telephone and Water provision too. Until you get a feel for things you might just want to take over the existing supply for different services so I would suggest that you arrange this before you move out. To this end you will find suppliers that have English speaking helplines a real bonus and we moved knowing that we had assured continuation of supply of electricity, telephone and internet. Two useful numbers here (note the French way of stating telephone numbers is in blocks of 2) are:

  EDF   +33 (0)5 62 16 49 08
  Orange +33 (0)9 69 36 39 00

3.3 Re-plug where practicable

In France the electricity supply runs at 230 volts rather than the 240 volts in the UK though you will still find that your appliances work satisfactorily whereas for emigrants from the USA things are more problematic as their supply runs at 120 volts so many of their appliances will not work. On the

So You're Thinking of Moving to France

other hand if your appliance is rated for example as 220-240v or indeed 110-240v then it will work automatically.

However the plug sockets and the plugs in France are totally different being essentially two pin, with (Type E) or without (Type C) an earth. You can either plan to use a travel adaptor and it is probably worth stocking up with a few of these in the first instance, or if you can obtain some French plugs you could re-plug those items/appliances for immediate use such as a Hoover, Kettle, Lamp or TV etc before arrival to smooth that first day.

3.4 Educate and Inform

People move for many reasons. If you intend setting up a business from scratch or utilising your existing skills in France or even taking over an existing business like a bar, *Chambres d'hôte* or *Gite* complex then why not use the time before you move to make sure you are aware of the relevant health and safety aspects, laws and regulations that will govern your new enterprise along with the tax implications, as they will undoubtedly be different to what you have been used to. For example, even if you want to offer B&B from your house you have to declare same at the *Mairie* using the appropriate CERFA (*centre d'enregistrement et de révision des formulaires administratifs*) form. Cerfa is a public body that was created to setup and amend all official documents. **However should you be thinking of opening as a Chambre D'hôte or indeed running any other business activity from your new home then be sure to understand the Capital Gains Tax implications when you sell it.**

Make sure that your skills and/or qualifications are readily transferable to the French marketplace or undertake/book the relevant training course(s) as necessary. If you are looking to open a business then look into acquiring some business French before you arrive so that you can converse with your likely clientele. As opening hospitality related businesses seems prevalent amongst Britons relocating to France, why not look to obtain some relevant knowledge before you move if you don't have any as learning on the job is not easy.

So You're Thinking of Moving to France

If you are opting to start a business don't let your heart or more importantly the sun rule your head. Without intentionally knocking anyone's entrepreneurial spirit I am staggered when watching TV programmes about people escaping to the continent to start a new life and/or business as to how many of them just stumble along without a clear plan. Seemingly happy to commit their life savings, or all the money they have made on a UK sale, into a new venture without any clear focus let alone anything like a contingency plan. It seems pretty certain that most of them act on a whim, seemingly devoid of any common sense.

You have potentially come to France to retire so ask yourself, 'do you have the time, energy and commitment to run a business'? Undertake some proper market research as a bare minimum, either before or after you arrive and then decide. Even though you may be funding your business with valuable equity made on your English sale rather than through a mortgage or bank loan, don't let it burn a hole in your pocket. Imagine you did need to apply for a mortgage or bank loan, would your idea be sufficiently well developed to get one? Draft a solid business plan and ideally let someone who is business minded impartially review it for you, rather than blindly assume that just because you open the business customers will flock towards you or there is a gap in the market. Ideally your business model should not rely on a single source/income stream and you need to ascertain what Return on your Investment is acceptable to you? It seems that many people haven't got a clue.
N.B. See section 6.41 if you are planning to let out property.

Some final words of warning and I can't stress enough, as is said in IT, draw up a [proper] plan [for launching your new venture] or plan to fail. At the same time don't give yourself impossible deadlines [for completing a renovation say and/or setting an opening date for a business] you don't need the added pressure particularly it is of the financial kind. Having to open by an arbitrary date to start cash flowing might motivate you at the outset but is not a great recipe for a quality build.
When setting timescales for opening your new business do remember that in this digital age it only takes a bad or scathing review to set you back and potentially finish you before you have started. So don't let your

So You're Thinking of Moving to France

hard work and possibly your dream go to waste, it simply isn't worth rushing things.

3.5 Opening a Bank Account

By and large and certainly based on our experience opening a French Bank account requires an awful lot more paperwork than in England in terms of ID Documents, Proof of Address and Income etc. so I would strongly suggest that you start to set one up as soon as is practicable.

We chose the worst possible time, two weeks before we downsized and the day before we flew out on our first viewing trip. At least we spoke to the Bank in person at a French Property show but this timing put added pressure on ourselves to open our Account with an English address while we still had various documentary evidence linking us to it.

It didn't help that the queries they had arose while we were away viewing properties and so there was an inbuilt delay in us responding. It also didn't help that they had not seen/opened all the attachments I had put on an email so into the second week while we were back home supervising our packing there were repeated requests from them for material I had already sent them. We suspect that pointing them to the earlier mail (and its associated attachments obviously helped our cause) and things went pretty smoothly after that.

Somewhat different to the UK we then had to arrange a time for a telephone interview from a Customer Service advisor before the account was fully opened but that may just be specific to our particular bank not all of them.

3.6 Budget

From your viewing trip(s) or holidays you will gain an idea of what certain everyday items cost. As you would expect some things will be cheaper than you are used to and others more expensive. So it is a good idea to try and draw up a monthly budget for everyday expenditure so you can keep an eye on your cashflow once you have moved and will help you plan your money transfers (See section 6.19). It goes without saying that

So You're Thinking of Moving to France

you are liable to spend more when you have guests staying with you (particularly If any of them have specific dietary needs) and you will certainly have plenty of those during the early months/years but also allow for increased expenditure during the summer months. Simply because the days are longer, more things are open, you will be inclined to get out and about more and, depending on the area you live, Summer [Night] markets abound and it is generally a far more sociable time.

I would also add a word of caution if you are planning to operate and receive income from letting *Gites*. You may be surprised but the season is a lot shorter than you might imagine and possibly will not extend much beyond July and August at the outset. If it does, fantastic, if it doesn't then that could blow a large hole in your monetary projections. Equally you may find that 'out of season' hires for a couple/three days at a time appear attractive but once you have factored in extra cleaning, laundry and possibly heating costs that these are potentially more trouble than they are worth!

⚠️ Also any requests for lengthy out of season hires may not be compatible with your licensing, you should take time to check!

3.7   Make necessary Purchases

As you will know the type and size of house you are moving from (in the UK) and what you are moving to why not take advantage of the time you have until the move completes to purchase any big item that you know you will needy e.g. a new bed, a mower, sofa's or washing machine? Notwithstanding my comments about shopping locally (See section 5.6 below) unless you plan to buy over the internet once you arrive it will likely take time for you to become familiar with the surrounding commerce and what is where in your new surroundings, so why not simply acquire anything big before you move? That gives you the benefit of
a) using your native language so to do; and
b) the possibility of getting any items transported to France by your removal company;
that way any stress caused by not having the item(s) in question

So You're Thinking of Moving to France

immediately available from Day 1 is eliminated. Plus you won't blindly rush into buying something that may prove to be sub-standard.

3.8   Other

Other practical considerations before setting off on your new life will include simple things like remembering to read your [Electricity, Gas & Water] meters before you move, forwarding your mail and advising family, friends and certain organisations of your new address, getting your animals micro-chips and passports sorted out etc.

If 'the One' has grounds as such or at least some acreage then consider buying a flashing collar for your dog(s). Your canine companion(s) will want to explore and get used to their new environment too and these collars are ideal for keeping an eye on their whereabouts when you let them out after dark.

Similarly we found it extremely useful to obtain a pair of walkie talkies. That way if one of you gets up early and goes into a barn to do some work or for a walk around the garden or woods then at least they are contactable. Equally if one is off doing some work during the day then they minimise a lot of wasted effort in walking backwards and forwards.

So You're Thinking of Moving to France

4. The Move

4.1 Logistics (What & When)

Once you know for certain that you are moving to France then you need to line up your removal company, although you may well have got some outline quotations in advance to help with your overall financial planning. Your agent or *Notaire* should be able to say what dates it will be possible to sign the *Acte de Vente* which will enable you to plan accordingly. For example depending on how much work you deem immediately necessary at your new property you may be intending to book into a local hotel for a few nights at the time of the move. All of these factors will enable you to discuss possible dates with your removal company, beware of Bank Holidays, both English and French (See section 5.11) as these may impact your expectations, or cost you more.

Do you know where you are moving to? Strange question I know but at the time we downsized we were still thinking in terms of running a *Gite* business so kept all of the furniture from our 6 bedroom house on the basis that it would all come in handy. Moving it into our eventual 3 bedroom house with no *Gites* not only meant we had more items than we needed but we had paid to keep and insure them in the interim and they all had to be transported across the channel with us.

4.2 Storage

Potentially a hidden cost to your move. If you sell up in the UK before buying in France then even if you move into rented accommodation it is likely that some or all of your belongings will need to go into storage. The longer it then takes to complete your move and relocate the trickier it becomes both in financial and practical terms. The former because you have to continue paying for both storage and insurance therein and the latter because it is conceivable that you may need to get to things that you currently have stored.

Most of the International removal companies will provide you with storage as required but they will likely charge you to move your things into storage and then to remove them again prior to

So You're Thinking of Moving to France

delivery to your new home. So if it is relevant or practical so to do, thin them out by selling/donating them.

Also if you have had goods stored you will only be given 28-30 days to notify the removal company of any damage/loss. That means that once you have arrived you will have to progressively open every single box to check the contents, whether you can fit them inside your new residence or not.

4.3 Practicalities Pre-Arrival

You should find that as part of the Sales Process (See section 2.8) your Vendors should have had their fosse emptied, inspected and certificated as such, also if there is a woodburning stove(s) then they should have furnished you, ideally your *Notaire*, with a certificate of the last time it was/they were swept. Practically both things may have been overlooked, deliberately or otherwise, so you may need to arrange these for when you have moved in.

International removal trucks tend to be bigger than average, make sure that there is enough room for them to both swing in and to enter your driveway, you don't want to complicate your life by having the removal men carry everything up from the road to the house, you want them parked directly outside the front door.

4.4 Insurance

Your removal company will presumably be insuring your possessions whilst they are in storage and/or during the move itself. But it is advisable to sort out your insurance before you move as you will be much too busy once you arrive. In case you weren't aware French House Insurance is a little different to that in the UK.

4.4.1 Accidental Damage

Probably most importantly there is no such thing as accidental damage/ all risks cover, unlike the UK. So if you drop a hammer/screwdriver on the sink or the television falls off the wall it's tough and down to you to replace!

So You're Thinking of Moving to France

4.4.2 Cancellation

Also there are differences as regards cancellation because one cannot be uninsured in France. If you have a policy with a company you have to give 2 months written notice to cancel it rather than just ring up before renewal like we were used to doing. However should you wish to change to a more competitive company they can effect the change for you without waiting the 2 months as they contact the extant company directly on your behalf.

4.4.3 Car Insurance

The principal difference here is that your car is insured not you as the driver. Advantageously in some respects, anyone driving your car with your permission is automatically covered by your insurance.

4.5 Logistics Post Move

Depending on how long it is between your English sale and French purchase you may well have accumulated some additional goods and chattels that ideally you want with you in your new home. If you plan to drive across this may be your answer, however if you are flying out or you have more than a car load what do you do? You can try and get your removal company to include them, at an acceptable cost, or you could consider one of the many companies that advertise carrying part loads.

A cautionary note here, with 6 months between our two dates we took the part load option. Most companies seem to base their quote on the volume of space that you are occupying in their vehicle. I chose a company that advertised frequent trips to France then diligently measured everything that we wanted to move and accepted their quote. Despite some communication difficulties on the day our additional goods were picked up the day before we were to fly out to start our adventure. So far so good. A couple of days later I was advised by phone there was a problem. The company then said that our boxes exceeded their weight limits (which hitherto had not been mentioned) and I had to pay extra. Finding out in these circumstances mean that they 'had me over a barrel' and I had no option but to pay up. I had planned to complain to Trading Standards but getting involved in lengthy correspondence when one is in the middle of moving and checking that everything else had been

So You're Thinking of Moving to France

received from storage satisfactorily was imperfect timing so I put it down to experience.

To avoid the same situation arising I would therefore urge you read any small print and/or pose the question as to whether the charges are based purely on volume or whether weight is involved too? That way you will avoid any nasty surprises.

That said however I separately and subsequently agreed a price to transport my ride-on mower across, based on size and weight, with a different company and had no problems whatsoever.

4.6   Dogs & Cats

If you are planning to bring your pet dog or cat to France then they will need their own individual pet passport, which unlike those for their owners is valid for the life of the pet. Note that different rules apply if the animal is less than 3 months old. Otherwise they basically need to be micro-chipped, have been injected against Rabies *Rage* at least 21 days prior to travel and have had a blood test to show that the vaccine is present in their system.

France is very dog friendly in that despite there being some awful stories about people abandoning their dogs when going on holiday I have not yet met a restaurant (including Michelin recommended ones) that didn't allow you to bring your 4 legged friend inside.

Just a plea from me, if you are thinking of rescuing/adopting a dog, don't think of getting one from say Rumania, although what happens there is truly shocking, there are many beautiful souls here in France just looking for their forever home. But again remove your rose-tinted spectacles. They will be in a dog pound *fourrière* or charity premises for a reason so you should be prepared to work through any behavioural issues that may arise with integrating them into their new home rather than assume everything will be 'hunky dory' from Day 1.

So You're Thinking of Moving to France

5. Settling In

There are various steps you can take to settle into both retirement (if that is what you are doing) and your new way of life and I attempt to list out some of them below, with what I deem the important ones first.

5.1 Settling into Retirement

There are lots of resources available that help one transition from a working life to retirement and I won't seek to replicate those here. What I will say is that every time I come back to the UK to visit family or friends I cannot imagine having retired in the UK.

Why? Probably the same routine, other than physically going to work, you are travelling the same streets, going to the same shops, seeing the same people and doing many of the same things as you previously did. It just wouldn't seem any different to me. Having a complete change of scenery and lifestyle certainly has helped me adjust to retirement far easier than I imagined. Certain habits are hard to break and I still list out tasks for the week in MoSCoW fashion, only I don't beat myself up if they are not done, there is always tomorrow; and I don't usually watch TV before the evening, unless it is the weekend.

Despite the change of scene and far less stress I still feel somewhat 'guilty' if for example I spend the morning reading, there is a little voice inside my head, or perhaps it's Joanne(!) that nags away saying I should be doing something so I guess I haven't got retirement completely cracked yet. I thought I would be bored retiring here which is why we originally thought about having a business to run but far from it, our social life is far better here than it was in the UK, principally because every day is a weekend and you are not just tied to Fridays/Saturdays for entertaining, so why not Monday night? Lunchtimes come into play too, far more than they ever did because a lot of your new friends will be in the same position and you are not inconveniencing anyone.

I believe that you can help yourself by having a number of (non House related) projects to look forward to. In my case that has been picking up my genealogy research again after 20 years, looking forward to digitising my extensive album collection, slowly

So You're Thinking of Moving to France

sorting out cataloguing and tagging my digital photos which have expanded exponentially and are stored haphazardly, similarly editing and putting finishing touches to various videos and becoming proficient in Photoshop. Ok so these are interior and PC centric projects but they could equally be exterior, depending on one's available budget, e.g. going to the major tourist attractions in the area (where you will have the advantage of being able to visit out of season when it is less crowded), trying out new restaurants, photography, cycling (which is extremely popular in France), getting involved in something in your commune etc.

Get involved in clubs or societies, ideally those that are not just expat focused. My longer-term projects aside I co-run a monthly lunch club (mainly for expats but with a sprinkling of French and Dutch as well) which generally meets on the last Wednesday of each month, depending on the restaurant. So there are always reconnaissance visits to look forward to, arrangements to make (in French) email invitations to draft and having *Menu du Jour/Menu Ouvriers* somewhere.

Also a friend recently persuaded me to go along to a weekly bowls club with him, nothing too serious and I never did anything like this in England so the game was somewhat alien to start with but after a couple of weeks I got the hang of it. But it is just as much about getting involved with a different circle of people (including some French couples) and socialising for a couple of hours a week as it is for the 'sport'. Unexpectedly a number of this new circle are heavily into rugby too which is a real bonus for me, and when it comes to actual sport however I go and actively watch the local rugby teams which gives me great enjoyment.

On a final note one should not underestimate the change in dynamics from just being with your husband/partner/wife on a 24 hour, 7 day a week basis. Something which apart from holidays very few of us experience before retirement. It will require a period of adjustment from you both but I can assure you it is well worth it.

So You're Thinking of Moving to France

5.2   The Maire

It is always advised in various moving-in guides that, if nothing else then out of politeness, one should go to say hello *'Bonjour'* to the local *Maire* after you have arrived in your new house. I would strongly endorse this move as you never know when you may require their services for one thing and another and to just turn up because you want things from them may not sit well. That said it took us 5 attempts to see our *Maire.* We first went along the week after we settled in but his secretary said he was on holiday. Time then intervened and we returned to the UK in the interim to collect our dog amongst other things but I did email him with some questions though in advance of our meeting.

The second time we thought about meeting him the morning ran away with us and we drove down at around 1145 only to be met by a large funeral procession coming up the road from the church which is opposite the *Mairie.* Out of politeness and respect I stopped the car and switched off the engine to let them past, then it occurred to us that he may be in the cortege walking after the coffin and we didn't know what he looked like as his picture was not on the commune website so we curtailed that visit. Attempt 3 on the following Friday saw us arrive at the *Mairie* only to be told he was very busy! We went back the following morning but he wasn't working that day. I think that they then felt sorry for us as they said to come mid-morning on the Monday. Attempt 5 was partially successful. Yes we met him and introduced ourselves but an administration hitch meant that when I mentioned the questions I had sent him he disappeared and we heard raised voices outside as it appeared he had not been given a copy. He apologised profusely, answered a couple of questions immediately and made an appointment for Wednesday the next week when he said he would have all the answers. He was true to his word although he had to telephone me personally when he needed to defer the appointment to the Thursday whereupon to his credit he did answer all outstanding questions.

Since then he has had far more interaction with us than any local official in the UK ever did. Coming to see us the day after a big storm to check

So You're Thinking of Moving to France

whether we had power and whether we had lost any trees or fences. He makes a point of coming over and shaking hands if we see him when we are out and about or attend a commune function, it's lovely. Also he was most apologetic and came in person to say that he could not come to our One Year On Moving in Party.

> **Hereafter the sections are in Alphabetical Order.**

5.3   Armistice & VE Day

Both of these events are public holidays in France and local communities place great store in the ceremonies that take place around the commune war memorial. In our village with regard to the Armistice it is preceded by a procession from the Cemetery to the memorial. On both occasions though the *Maire* gives a small speech and usually part of it involves children from the local school. Specially erected loudspeakers then play *Le Marseillaise* and everyone is then invited to retire to the *Salle de Fêtes* /*Salle Polyvalente* to partake in a *Vin d'honneur* at a small wine reception. Depending on your target location in France, Resistance memorial events are another good way to be seen in the community. Be visible in your new surroundings, participate in these events and become known to your new neighbours, one day some of them will become your friends.

5.4   Chasse

Whether one condones it or not the local hunt *Le Chasse* is part of weekly life in rural France. When I say hunt I am not talking about scarlet clad riders on large horses, more men on foot in high-visibility jackets with shotguns and accompanied by dogs. There are strict seasons (usually all in the Autumn-Winter) for the hunting of different types of animal, boar *sanglier*, deer *chevreuil*, foxes *les renards* etc. and the hunters *Chasseurs* actively pursue them most weekends in season.

The thought of the *Chasse* hunting across our land with, at the time, one dog, and the possibility of Grandchildren out playing was too much so when we moved in one of the questions we asked the *Maire* was the contact details for the President of the local *Chasse*. I wrote to him explaining same and asking them not to come anywhere near our

So You're Thinking of Moving to France

property. I also put up signs, purchased at the local DIY store saying *Chasse Interdite* (Hunting Forbidden) around the boundary.

Although we had seen and heard them from time to time we didn't have too much of a problem although we generally didn't venture into the garden on Saturday mornings; there have been too many shooting accidents reported for that to feel comfortable. Consequently it was something of a surprise when sitting in our kitchen one sunny September Saturday two *Chasseurs*, one with a shotgun, appeared out of the trees on the boundary at the bottom of the garden and started to walk around the *Etang* and into our woods. By the time I had got my boots on to go down there 2 dogs had appeared as well. Now our dogs are fiercely territorial but I didn't dare let them out with me for fear of what might happen. When I caught up with them I told them in no uncertain terms it was private property and they had to leave, which they reluctantly did.

Cutting a long story short I got the name of the current President of the *Chasse* from the *Mairie*, wrote a complaint to him and copied the *Maire* and the local Gendarmerie Commandant. When I didn't get a response the *Maire* got involved and directed the *Chasse* to respond. I then had a visit from their secretary who spoke perfect English, albeit with an American accent, and I explained what happened. It appeared the *Chasseurs* had said they only went into our garden after their dogs! He was candid and said that if historically people had hunted on certain areas of land they would tend to ignore any signs that then appeared. However in their Meeting Room he said there was a large map of the commune that showed all the *Parcelles* within it (See section 2.5 above for more information), he asked me to write to him personally with details of the relevant *Parcelle* numbers for our property and he would ensure their map was marked accordingly. On a point of clarification he said that *Les Chasseurs* should not hunt on our land but if they had shot something elsewhere which subsequently came into it they were allowed to follow 'to finish it. Enough said!

The law states that *Chasseurs* are not allowed to venture within 150m of a house with a loaded weapon, however, as my French teacher said to me 'there is the law and there is everyday France'.

So You're Thinking of Moving to France

5.5 Emergency Phone Numbers

When moving to a new environment it is very important to know how to get help should you need it. Programme these numbers into your house phone and your mobiles and make sure that your children know them too, and in their case make sure they learn their new address as you never know when they might need it.

In the first instance call

17	Police and Gendarmerie
18	All other emergencies You will connect to the fire brigade (*Sapeurs Pompiers*) they will also deal with small scale medical emergencies and should be your first port of call (if necessary they will contact *SAMU*)
114	Emergency Calls (Hearing Assisted or if you cannot talk you can communicate by text)
15	SAMU (*Le service d'aide médicale urgente*) If you have an urgent medical emergency

Other useful numbers

196	Coastguard,
119	Report Child Abuse
116 000	Report missing child
112	Universal European Emergency Services number works from all phones including mobiles
116 117	Out of hours Doctors
3237	Outside hours GP and pharmacy information

In addition

09 726 750 dd	Gas & electricity emergencies + your department number (eg 19 for Coreze)
01 46 21 46 46	English speaking SOS helpline

So You're Thinking of Moving to France

5.6 Integration

As well as Armistice and VE Day there are lots of local events in your commune that you will see advertised, be they Dances, Meals, Rambles or Quizzes. Join in and be visible rather than aloof.

Use your local commerce where you can. I appreciate it is all too easy to pop to the Supermarket for your weekly shop but try and spend something in your local Bar, *Boucherie, Boulangerie, Pharmacie* or Restaurant. So many French villages have lost their commerce as people have moved away and trade has slowed down to such an extent that it is uneconomic to remain open, just like a lot of towns and villages in the UK, but unless you want to live in one of those ghost towns give them some of your business on a regular basis.

A good source of contacts, clubs or information about your new area is the Internet. Key 'expats in <name of your *Département*>' into your preferred search engine and a host of contact information will be displayed which you can then follow up on.

Obviously if you have a dog(s) it maybe you want to walk them regularly to help with their claws or just to get to know your new neighbourhood? Being out and about you will start to see some regular faces be they fellow residents or the local farmers and they will get to know you too and this is an ideal way of integrating into your new community. After a while you may start to have a [limited] conversation with them, it all depends on how good your French is or how confident you are.

5.7 Internet Access

The internet and access to it are very much an integral part of everyday life and as part of moving in you will probably want to include internet access along with obtaining a telephone service. Nationally the current administration has some grand ambitions for all houses to be able to access 'very fast broadband' *Très Haut Débit* (30Mbps or more) by 2022, and they want 80% of this to be supplied through fibre optic connections.

So You're Thinking of Moving to France

Whereas it seems that all *Départements* are planning to just service the major cities, towns and possibly large villages, the Correze has announced that it intends to deliver *Très Haut Débit* to **every household** in every commune by 2021. An unexpected bonus for us as we were completely unaware of this prior to moving.

5.8 Loyalty Cards

Most of the supermarkets here have their own loyalty cards *cartes de fidélité* although rather than collect points (think Clubcard or Nectar) their rewards are generally in cash which you redeem against shopping. Their schemes aren't always as comprehensive as in the UK in that you can collect across other stores in the chain but only redeem in the one where you opened the account. Some give discounts on fresh fruit and veg' once you have shopped so many times in a month and generally they all run 'Promo's' on certain goods, so when you buy them it puts so much money back on your card. You sometimes pay a little more for the product but get the excess refunded on your card so in that way they can act like a savings scheme if you want them to.

By and large these cards are very good value in that you can easily accumulate low three figure sums throughout the year to offset against your Christmas shop say or to acquire an otherwise costly domestic product. Most schemes are based on a collection year but there is one supermarket that just rolls it over. Check at your local store.

In addition you may find that at different times of the year certain chains also have wider promotions, giving stickers/vouchers for say every 10€ spent in store for which you can obtain a branded product once you have collected so many. These seem great value as in the past couple of years we have acquired Masterchef kitchenware, Picnic Glasses, Pyrex Dishes with covers, Villeroy & Boch Knives, and Wooden Chopping Boards as an added bonus by doing just that; but we declined collecting towels and dressing gowns as they were too expensive. However should you be looking to furnish a *Gite*(s) then this is a way of reducing the cost.

So You're Thinking of Moving to France

One word of warning, show your card to the cashier when they are scanning your goods for rewards to be reconciled to your account. Unlike the UK showing it afterwards or even taking your receipt and card to Customer Services after you have paid will not get your points/rewards allocated, their systems are just not setup for it.

I have also subscribed to a couple of DIY Store loyalty schemes but in two years or more despite spending four figure sums there I have never received anything other than an invite to a promotional evening so would not recommend rushing to obtain one of these.

5.9   Opening Hours

In the rural parts of France and indeed some towns do not be surprised to see that local commerce sometimes shuts all day on a Monday. In addition it is highly likely that many shops will close for a couple of hours at some point between 12.00pm and 3.00pm each day for lunch.

5.10   Petrol Stations

In the UK we are used to seeing service stations as part of the major supermarkets as well as along the highway (and indeed some more rural roads too). Invariably they will all have a shop of some kind associated with them where you can stock up on supplies for the journey or even do the day's shopping if you need to. Here in France however it is somewhat different.

Yes some of the large supermarkets have an associated Petrol Station (where one generally pays at a kiosk rather than in a shop) but 'Pay at the Pump' is uncommon, usually reserved for out of hours service and restricted to one or two pumps.

What you will also find different is that again you may be used to stations having Air and Water supplies, some free some payable. Again in France this is a rarity so it is best to have at least a foot pump in the boot of the car or alternatively one of those 'plug in' compressors that work off the 12v socket on the dashboard just in case.

So You're Thinking of Moving to France

5.11 Public Holidays

It is often commented that France has far more Public/Bank Holidays than the UK, and indeed it does with 11 in all *Départements* with an additional 2 in Alsace and Moselle. However there are two distinct differences with the UK as regards Pubic Holidays in that:

a. It is not uncommon for the date to fall midweek, in which case the holiday will take place then, rather than the next Monday. (If it is a Tuesday/Thursday French working families will often make a long weekend of it *Faire Un Pont* by utilising the Monday/Friday to have a 4 day break; and
b. If the date falls on a weekend then unlike the UK the Monday will not automatically become a Bank Holiday.

See Annex C and Annex D for details of holidays in 2019-2020.

5.12 Septic Tank

If you are planning to move to a large City or Town then this guide may not be overly useful to you but if you are moving to a small village somewhere in rural France or indeed to the countryside itself then it is likely that you will not be connected to mains sewage and that your flushable household waste is accumulated on site in a Septic Tank *Fosse Septique*.

I suspect that the majority of readers will not have encountered one of these before, it being a concrete or more likely plastic chamber sited underground through which said waste passes fed by gravity. Basically the waste is then treated anaerobically (i.e. without air), the solids sink to the bottom and reduce in size and the liquid ultimately drains out through a runoff into the soil. Even if you don't know the location of this 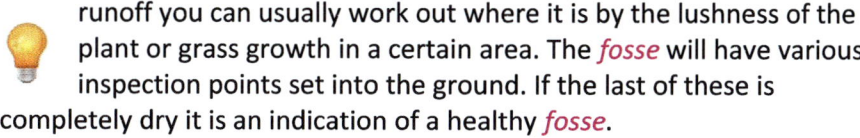 runoff you can usually work out where it is by the lushness of the plant or grass growth in a certain area. The *fosse* will have various inspection points set into the ground. If the last of these is completely dry it is an indication of a healthy *fosse*.

5.12.1 Legalities

It is estimated that up to 80% of homes in rural areas rely on a Fosse and it is the commune's responsibility to ensure they don't become health or

So You're Thinking of Moving to France

environmental hazards and enforce the strict regulations that apply. Most do this through *SPANC (Service Public d'Assainissement Non Collectif)*, a national body (See Annex B). Legally each system needs to be checked every 10 years but if you are selling your house you are required to have your *Fosse* emptied before the sale.

5.12.2 Problems

For those of you new to having your house use a Septic Tank, be aware that you sometimes get a foul smelling sewer type odour when it rains, this may be because:
- If it is cold, it may cause a downdraft as such from your vent stack which disappears as the temperature warms up or it may vary during the day due to wind direction
- Frequently when it rains, atmospheric pressure changes and air becomes heavier meaning that the methane gases that are in the tank don't flow through the vent as they would normally do. Instead, they remain lower to the ground and this causes a foul smell, like the rotten eggs you will remember from school chemistry lessons.
- The vent system in the tank may have become blocked. This can happen if there has been work done on your house or in the garden adjacent to it and if the vents aren't working then the sewage gases can't escape from the wastewater.

For the unknowledgeable it is important to note that only material produced by the human body should enter your septic tank. That means no Baby Wipes, Cotton Buds, Cotton Wool, Feminine Hygiene products, Kitchen Roll or Tissues should be flushed down the toilet. You will find *fosse* tolerant toilet paper and other *fosse* compatible products eg bleach at your local supermarket. Don't make the mistake that we did initially in flushing tissues and kitchen roll 'down the loo' as you will overpower the *fosse* and find that your house becomes full of nasty smells.

Should you think that your *fosse* is not working properly don't despair, there are *fosse* cleaners or re-energiser/additive products that are available from the supermarket or specialist companies.

So You're Thinking of Moving to France

5.13 Setting up Direct Debits

Once you have setup a Bank Account it then becomes much easier to pay for things because you just show/give a copy of your *RIB* (*Relevé d'Identité Bancaire*) to the organisation/company in question. Basically the *RIB* is your statement of identity that contains account details:

- The *nom* and *prenom* (s) or business name of the account holder;
- The bank code (5 digits);
- The counter code (5 digits);
- Account number (11 digits or letters);
- RIB key (2 digits);
- the title of the institution and the counter holding the account;
- For international account identification: the IBAN code (International Bank Account Number) a series of numbers and letters (27), including the bank code and the account number, and
- the Business Identifier Code (BIC) (11 or 8 digits or letters).

and it then becomes relatively straightforward to setup Direct Debits etc using it.

The *RIB* may also contain optional information (this depends on the practices of the institutions) such as the account holder's address and the address and telephone number of the bank counter.

 Some organisations will accept photocopies of these but you will find 'formal' spares in the back of your chequebook if you need them.

5.14 Television

A lot of people moving to France will have concerns that they will not be able to use their UK Televisions or they miss out on their favourite TV shows (as by reputation French TV is awful).

5.14.1 Setup

The good news is that if your television is rated for 230 Volts it will work in France albeit with a different plug. I don't have any personal experience but I believe that older Freeview boxes will likely not work here although you can purchase newer equipment in most supermarkets

So You're Thinking of Moving to France

and use it to pick up the French equivalent TNT (*La télévision numérique terrestre*) channels.

If you have a satellite dish it is possible to align it to the Astra Satellite and pick up the Sky TV you may be familiar with, even though they don't have a licence to broadcast in France. The rule of thumb here is that the further south in the country you are the bigger the dish you need. Geographically we are located around 45°N and our 80cm dish works fine. One thing you will find in newspapers & magazines, particularly those directed towards an expat audience is adverts for TV installers. Similarly you will find a number of companies who will supply you with a full Sky package of your choosing.

5.14.2 Sky by Broadband
In 2017 Sky announced that it will soon be offering its full TV service of nearly 300 channels via broadband, without the need for a satellite dish for the first time (although no release date was announced).

While its Customers can currently use the Now TV broadband service to watch a limited range of Sky channels without a dish that service is only available for UK residents, and roaming abroad (including France) is only available for 30 days at a time. After that, one needs to confirm one is still a UK resident by watching NOW TV back in the UK before you can watch abroad again, but it may be possible to watch through a VPN.

5.14.3 Sports, well Rugby Union
If you are a sports fan like I am and follow the oval ball game then you will find that there are other ways to watch:
- The French channel FR2 streams all French National Team matches, along with those in the Champions/Heineken Cup.
- The French subscription channel Canal+ shows French Top 14 rugby
- Eurosport shows matches in Pro D2 – second tier French rugby.

You can pick up FR2 by streaming the games from their website whereas you can subscribe to Eurosport player or Canal+ for a preferred period of time and view matches this way in full HD on your computer.

So You're Thinking of Moving to France

5.15 Traps

In this section I am not writing about catching animals, although that may be a concern depending on where you live and what animals you keep, e.g. chickens *poulets*, goats *chèvres* or sheep *mouton*. (We had a particular problem with Coypu *ragondin* which necessitated actual traps) no, this is about the everyday traps to avoid if you want a successful integration into your new life.

This is about the everyday traps to avoid if you want a successful integration into your new life.

5.15.1 English Language

Obviously when one moves to a new environment it gives comfort to be able to have some degree of normality and so it is easier to make English friends (although see my caveat below) and speak English all the time when you see them. This is reassuring but does not help learning your new language and, in many cases, detracts from it. Try to limit your English exposure and tune into local radio in the car and the kitchen and watch French Television shows if you are able. Quiz programmes are generally easy to follow even if you don't know all the answers.

5.15.2 Friends

Each to their own of course but we made a conscious decision before we arrived that we would not go out of our way to make friends with people just because they were English. Our view was if it was unlikely we would befriend them in England then why would we in France? Better to try and expand one's horizons and meet and get to know the French, Belgian or Dutch nationals that live locally.

5.15.3 Food

Yes it is relatively easy to obtain most types of English food. There are travelling 'tuck shops' and most supermarkets have an International section but they come at a price. If that is a price you are prepared to pay then so be it but surely one of the delights of moving to France is to sample the different types of cuisines and delicacies. To have a 3, 4 or 5 course *Menu du Jour* with accompanying Wine and Coffee and not pay through the nose so to do. There are also approximately 300 varieties of

So You're Thinking of Moving to France

cheese to work your way through. If you ask a foreign national to name an English dish they will invariably say 'Fish and Chips' yet in naming a French dish you easily get into double figures. Try them out!

5.15.4 Translation

Making word for word translations into English doesn't work in every instance and can greatly confuse you. Unfortunately, there is no real substitute for learning French idioms, Phrases and Sayings and then introducing them into your everyday conversation.

5.16 Wiring & Electricity

5.16.1 Electricity Supply

When you buy your French property you are able to stipulate the kilowattage of electricity supply you require, in other words the power rating for your meter (*puissance de compteur*). This is usually set at one of the following levels: 6kw, 9kw, 12kw or 15kw and your standing charges will reflect this, these levels being the amount of power that your household will draw from the National Grid. There are plenty of online resources out there to help you calculate this.

5.16.2 Wiring

As you may know the wiring system in UK houses is significantly different to those in France. The former is based on a ring main i.e. a circular system with sockets effectively chained together whereas the latter uses a radial or star system with the Fuse Board *Tableau* at the centre and circuits emanating from separate fuses within it. Thus any budding 'DIYers' amongst you need to take particular care to understand what you are working with before rushing into putting extra sockets in. It is best to consult a qualified electrician.

So You're Thinking of Moving to France

6. Everyday Living

Once you have settled into life in France you can start to appreciate the different aspects of living that drew you here in the first place. There are so many different features to this that I will not attempt to prioritise them as everyone will have their own sequence, and merely list them in alphabetical order.

6.1 Banking Cheques & Cash etc.

6.1.1 French Cheques

In the UK cheques had 5 separate components. The date, the payee, the amount in writing and then in figures and the signature. French cheques have 6 elements as they somewhat perversely also include the name of the place where the cheque was written. Further, rather than write the payee first then the amount you are paying them, on French cheques it is the reverse; one writes the amount first (in French obviously) with the payee on the line below.

6.1.2 Widespread Use of Chequebooks

Unlike the UK where they have been progressively phased out cheques are still in widespread use here in France where it is both illegal to write a cheque if there isn't sufficient money in the account to cover it and where if you do you will be likely blacklisted by your bank. Beware also the short queue in the supermarket, you may find that once everything is bagged up the customer then gets out a chequebook to pay and of course takes an age to sign it before the till takes an age to process it. Our local supermarket passes a cheque backwards and forwards through the till 10 times before the cashier shows it to the customer. Typically, customers do not write the whole cheque out, they just sign it and the till does the rest.

6.1.3 Account Alerts

As with accounts in the UK it is relatively easy to setup warning alerts on your account whereby you will receive an email or text message if your account balance falls below a certain threshold. However these are not always as instant as you would like/need.

So You're Thinking of Moving to France

Consequently I would suggest to start with set a higher value than you are used to.

6.1.4 Compte Nickel

If you want a simple 'low risk' bank account with the usual banking guarantees a '*Compte Nickel*' may be the answer. They were originally partly established to offer banking to people barred from other banks, no questions are asked. Nowadays anyone over 18 who is a French resident (with a residency permit) or has an EU passport (this includes holiday home owners) can open such an account at a local *Tabac* at the cost of just 20 € for an annual membership fee. The account opening process is straightforward, requiring only ID (such as a passport) and a working mobile phone number.

You get access to internet banking, online statements and a Mastercard debit card – but no cheques, and can take out money at any banks' cash dispensers showing the Mastercard symbol or other *tabacs* offering *Compte-Nickels*. You cannot go overdrawn because payments are not accepted above your balance. There are 25,000 *tabacs* in France and those participating in the scheme are evenly spread across the country.

6.2 Blood Doning

I have given blood since I was 18 and with everything I had heard about the nature of the French Healthcare System I thought I would be able to do the same once I'd moved. A couple of months after arriving I saw the banners advertising for donations in my local town. I went along and explained that I was a regular donor in the UK but they would not accept my donation. Seemingly if you have lived in the UK between 1980 and 1996 you cannot donate due to concerns arising from BSE! Perversely should you suffer a tragic accident your organs are acceptable to be donated! Consequently I have to try and fit in any continued donations during visits back to the UK, and that is not always possible with the NBTS appointment system that is in force.

6.3 Bonfires

You may think that you are perfectly at liberty to incinerate rubbish or garden waste at any time. You will be surprised as depending on your

So You're Thinking of Moving to France

Commune (and there are over 30,000 in mainland France) you may find for example that Bonfires are limited to between 1st October and 31st March. It may also be that you can only set these up in specific *Parcelles* depending on the number of them that your property consists of. As with all local matters you should check with your *Mairie* as to what is permissible, what isn't and when.

6.4   Cars

On our third viewing trip we drove our leased car over from England for the week and it suited us just fine. However it reinforced the idea that if we were going to be living here fulltime that we would need a left-hand drive car as it simply made more sense from a practical and safety perspective. Some of the local roads are quite narrow and driving 'on the wrong side' of the road definitely restricts your view as a driver and you are generally more reliant on your passenger, if you have one. For us it was also a commitment worth making as we intended making France our home so why would we buy/bring a right hand drive model over?

Indeed there are women that Joanne knows (all of whom have right hand drive cars) that do not like driving here and prefer to let their husbands do it as they do not feel safe nor confident. In which case the question has to be 'what will you do if anything happens to your husband'?

Those issues aside if you are staying in France for longer than six months (in any twelve month period), then French law requires that your car is formally registered here in France and plated with a French registration number. Naturally there will be a number of costs associated with this.

Whilst driving, if for example you get a bad puncture or one of your tyres wears out and you are looking to replace it then you need to be aware that in France to remain legal the two tyres on a single axle have to be the same brand and type, mixing and matching is not permitted.

6.5   Cashback

A regular feature of everyday life in the UK, usually in supermarkets but many different shops will offer this if you ask, providing you are using a

So You're Thinking of Moving to France

PIN entry to validate the transaction. In France however this is not an everyday occurrence and cashback is only offered In a very llmited number of places and at the time of writing this means Supermarkets or Hypermarkets in the Casino chain.

6.6   Churches

6.6.1   Church Bells

Irrespective of possibly marking of the hours, funerals and weddings you will find your village church bells will automatically ring out at certain times every day, a legacy from a far more religious time when the church bells sounded a call to prayers at:

   7.00 – for Matins
   12.00 – for Midday Prayer
   19.00 – for Vespers/evening prayer

and the bells were meant to be heard by everyone in the village, although nowadays it seems that the midday bells trigger a rush to the local restaurants by workmen keen to make a start on their *Menu Ouvriers* and shops start to close for business too.

There are some amusing stories around about the ringing of church bells in villages. In one locality apparently some Parisians had hired a nearby *Gite* and after a few days petitioned the *Maire* to get the bell ringing delayed as it was waking them up. Needless to say the *Maire* politely declined but amusingly mentioned that he could not do anything about the cockerels crowing either as it was the countryside after all.

6.6.2   Proximity to a Church

If your 'One' is situated close to a church you will not just have the ringing of the bells to contend with. There are various constraints on what you can and cannot do to your property if it is visible from the Church. This varies from place to place so it is best to make enquiries at the *Mairie* before you set your heart on doing something.

6.7   Cleaning Chimneys

If you have a woodburning stove(s) in your house it is usually a condition of your house insurance that these are swept annually. Your decision of course as in some areas finding a *ramoneur* is as rare as finding hen's

So You're Thinking of Moving to France

teeth but if you were unfortunate enough to have a chimney fire or some kind of fire with the stove identified as the cause then you can bet your life that your insurance company will ask you for a copy of the latest certificate. So my view is it is better to be safe than sorry.

6.8   Customer Service

In the UK we have been spoiled, 'the Customer is King' after all. Although we somewhat reluctantly step forward when it comes to making complaints about poor service or overcharging we now expect our complaints to be dealt with quickly and professionally. I do now suggest that you leave some of these pre-conceptions behind. The fact that you have complained, by email, in person, or through a website doesn't always mean you will get a speedy or indeed satisfactory response. It

may even to all intents and purposes be ignored. **Do not lose your cool.** It all ties in with a slower pace of life and a different mindset. Re-adjust your expectations, downwards!

6.9   Déchetteries

Recycling has improved a lot in France over recent years but one area that has not caught on is that of recycling food waste. It just goes in your dustbin with the rest of the household rubbish *ordures ménagères*.

So it is likely you will become familiar with the local dump or council tip as it is in the UK and the same exists in France where they are known as *déchetteries* (See Annex B for more information on locations etc).

They are just as organised as you have come to expect in the UK, with separate containers for some or all of Garden Waste, General Rubbish *déchet*, Glass, Hard Core, Metal, Paper, Plastic, Polystyrene, Wood etc. together with a specific area for old appliances. Generally they are only staffed by a single person who zealously maintains the cleanliness and order of their site as one would do in one's own workplace; so if you make a mess transferring rubbish from your car or trailer into the bin expect to clean it up, or you will be asked to do so. Equally do not expect them to give you a helping hand, it is not always forthcoming. Until you become familiar with the specific personnel, and vice versa, you will likely be asked which commune you have come from as they expect you to be

So You're Thinking of Moving to France

a local and you will be subjected to numerous questions if the *département* plate on your car does not correspond to the local area.

The usual opening times are 0900-1200 and 1400 to 1800 and they are not open on Sundays, although do check first. Like a lot of French workers their lunch time is sacrosanct. Before now we have arrived at a local *déchetterie* at 1145 and had to wait 10 minutes or so for a lorry to exchange an empty container for a full one only to then be told that we had to leave (before unloading) as it was closing at lunchtime.

6.10   Depot(s) de Pain

On average, France has some 35,000 bakeries and indeed it used to be the case that that every town was required by law to have a *boulangerie* (bakery). However, if a town or village is too remote, a *dépôt de pain* is allowed, where bread is made off-site and delivered fresh daily. As the name implies, a *dépôt de pain* is a place where bread is deposited & sold by a third party, this could be a local bar, hotel, restaurant, *tabac* etc.

Another alternative is whereby some *Boulangeries* will come to a nearby village in a van maybe a couple of times a week tooting their horn as they drive down the street and park up before selling their wares. If you are a fan of the baguette then you would do well to check out the potential *Boulangeries* /*Dépôts de Pain* in your search area.

6.11   DIY Stores

Think practically. Depending on your plans for 'the One' how close is the nearest DIY Store and is it likely to stock everything you need? Is it a few minutes in the car or up to half an hour away? Do you have the sort of car that will enable you to make and transport large purchases? If it is not very big and you don't have a trailer (See section 7.12) then you are looking at paying for delivery each time, and delivery in France is not cheap and would need to be factored into your budget for the work.

So You're Thinking of Moving to France

6.12 Etiquette

6.12.1 Official

As you will find when you initiate correspondence with the Health System as well as any Wedding Certificate they will also likely request a Birth Certificate in your wife's maiden name. Thereafter it is not unusual to receive official correspondence in the form of Mr <Married name> and Mrs <Maiden Name> or your wife to just receive letters in her maiden name. The Tax Office also refer to your wife by her maiden name on their correspondence and on your tax return as well.

6.12.2 Public

Despite their reputation as being rude the French people are actually very polite. People that you don't know, even groups of teenagers say hello *bonjour* to you as you meet them/are walking down the street and it is only courteous to reply in the same manner. Similarly when you enter a shop it is expected that you will say hello to the person serving so if they are not in front of you look around and direct your *bonjour madame/monsieur* to them, also say goodbye *au revoir* when you leave. Handshakes are not uncommon, either for the first time of meeting or seeing someone on a more regular basis. If there are mixed sexes present then *bonjour messieurs dames* or just *messieurs dames* will suffice, similarly if you meet a couple when you are out.

It seems that *Bonjour* can be replaced by *Bonsoir* around 5pm although one of my neighbours will still say *Bonjour* at 7/8pm if he sees me out with the dogs. Unlike in the UK Good Afternoon *Bonne Après-Midi* seems reserved for farewells rather than greetings.

Friends and family also kiss (*la bise ou bisous*) when greeting each other. The number of kisses range from two to even four depending on which part of the country you are in. By kisses I am just talking a light brush on the cheek whilst usually making a kiss sound rather than a real smacker! One falls into this approach quite quickly with the friends one makes but I have to say amongst our new circle of friends none of the (English) guys do it to each other!

So You're Thinking of Moving to France

However, once you have moved in it is unlikely that there will be a constant stream of neighbours beating a path to your door to introduce themselves it doesn't seem to be the French way, but you'll meet them in time.

6.13 Farmers Cooperative

Something that you may not initially consider as they are not particularly widespread in the UK is the nearest Farmers Cooperative *coopérative d'agriculteurs* (or sometimes just *agricole*) as a source of DIY products. Yes they can be agricultural in outlook but they will stock a wide range of e.g. Clothing, Electrical Items, Fencing, Paint, Plumbing Materials etc. and they are not as expensive as you might think and it could be that it is a lot closer to you than your nearest DIY store.

6.14 Fencing

Rigid wire/metal fence panels in Green, Grey or white are very common hereabouts and they have wide price differentials too. If you are budget conscious shop around by all means but don't assume that they are all [mounted] the same. Yes you have to concrete the posts into the ground but the fixing mechanism between post and panel differs depending on where you buy it, you can't mix and match. We bought as many panels as were in stock from a large DIY chain and got the balance from the *Brico* half of a local Hypermarket. Only when coming to use them did I find that they are totally incompatible so the Hypermarket stock had to be returned and we had to wait for the DIY store to be resupplied.

6.15 Gas Supply

If you cook with gas or have gas fired heating you are probably used to gas just being there through the mains. Not so in rural France. In towns you are ok but elsewhere you may find your cooker uses propane gas (and you can obtain the cylinders from the local garage or supermarket, some of which have installed automatic dispensers so they are available 24/7) and the gas for your heating comes from a tank which is sited in your garden, either above or below ground. So far so good.

So You're Thinking of Moving to France

However should you wish to change gas suppliers because you find you can get it cheaper elsewhere you could be in for a nasty financial shock, as it seems that the tank is not actually yours but is owned by the Gas supply company. Not too bad if your tank is above ground but if it is buried below ground you can be charged upwards of 500 € for them to come and remove it. What is more your new company will then charge you some 100 € or more to install one of their tanks. When you factor these hidden charges into the cost of supply you may well find that your new deal is not as an attractive proposition as it first appeared.

6.16   Health & Safety

You will find that France has not been overtaken by the pervasive Health and Safety culture that has become commonplace in the UK, so you will find that there are not as many constraints. It is amusing/scary watching sometimes for example when you see two ladders up against the front of a house and a horizontal plank placed between them on the ladder stays for a tradesman/builder to attend the roof. Joanne is convinced that I have adopted this *laissez-faire* attitude to my work but I think that is just because she times her arrival at my worksite as I am tripping over

a tool or extension lead that I had temporarily forgotten was there in my desire to complete the job.

6.17   Ivy

The ivy in our garden is quite prolific but for me it is parasitic and best left alongside holly at Christmas. It grows quite vigorously and when I see it strangling the life out of a majestic oak tree I just want it gone and so I have made it my mission these past 3 winters to slowly excise it from all the trees in our garden if at all possible. That is easier said than done as

So You're Thinking of Moving to France

 we are not talking a little snip with some secateurs, our ivy can be as thick as your arm when you have been weight training and generally needs both a chainsaw and crowbar to remove it. As well as any tools that you might choose to use for the job I would strongly recommend that you wear a hat and a mask, even eye protection if you have a sensitive disposition and possibly take an anti-histamine too to avoid any residual problems.

Reason being is that long established ivy gives off fumes/dust that can cause respiratory problems or sore throats, been there read the book, got the T-Shirt! For this reason you should not burn it either but take it to the *déchetterie* instead.

When you have achieved your objective in removing the ivy you will find something definitely satisfying about passing said tree some six months on and seeing it totally rejuvenated with new unencumbered growth.

6.18 Junk Mail

A curse as in any country. If you want to opt out of receiving large volumes of unsolicited post write *Pas de Pub(licité)* on your postbox.

6.19 Lavage/Laverie

This would be deemed an oddity in the UK as we have launderettes in towns but here it is possible to drive along and see a purpose-built housing usually containing a couple of washing machines (of differing capacities) and a tumble dryer either by the side of the road or in the vicinity of a supermarket. Often people deposit their washing/drying here, the wash cycles supply their own powder, set the machines running and pop off to the shops before returning at the end of the cycle to collect or dry their loads.

This may be entirely specific to our area as there are often large transient communities associated with equestrian events or apple picking in the local orchards who can take advantage of these permanent features.

13 June 2019

So You're Thinking of Moving to France

However if one has large quilts or multiple dog beds etc. these facilities are ideal for residents too.

6.20   Money Transfers

If you have attended any property shows or carried out any research at all about moving here then you should be aware that when it comes to buying a foreign property or making regular cost of living transfers it doesn't matter how helpful they are or what sort of relationship you have with them, do **not** use your bank for this service. Please use a Foreign Exchange broker as you will get a far far better rate.

Why? Some reasons being that it is not necessarily a banks prime specialism, you won't necessarily get a dedicated resource/contact to use, brokers work with different margins and can usually provide far better rates and brokers won't charge you fees to make the transfer. Many of them offer live exchange rate feeds that you can look at on your smartphone or laptop. If you don't believe me then make a couple of calls on varying potential amounts and compare the results.

N.b. Ensure the broker is regulated and find out how long their transfers will take before committing to anything.

Something also to consider if you are concerned about exchange rates fluctuating due to political and stock market influences, and certainly something that worked in our favour, is to secure a forward rate. That basically means that if you like the current exchange rate then you can secure that rate whilst buying a particular amount of currency in the future. Usually a 5-10% deposit is all that is needed. I secured a 4 month forward purchase to buy our house and by the time I actually transferred the money the rate had decreased 9.2%, happy days!

6.21   MOT's

The French equivalent of an MOT is the *Contrôle Technique* and it is applicable to all cars over 4 years old. There are differences to the UK system in that the tests are valid for 2 years but you will not be sent a reminder that it is due (and with a 135€ fine for non-attendance). As of May 2018 the test was made more stringent than previously as regards

So You're Thinking of Moving to France

vehicle safety and pollution control and there are now more than 600 control points as against over 450 previously.

There are 3 outcomes to the test. Success means that your log book *Carte Grise* is updated accordingly and you get a sticker for your windscreen which also states the date the next test is due.

Of the 2 types of failure, cars that don't pass are either classed as 'unfavourable' which means the owner has 2 months to get the necessary repairs made and to re-submit the car for a retest. Their *Carte Grise* is stamped with a letter S' to indicate this. If the faults are serious then the car is classed as 'critique' meaning that it cannot legally go back on the road until repaired. An 'R' sticker is placed on your windscreen and you are only able to use it on the road for the remainder of the day, except for being able to drive it to a garage for repair within 24 hours of the test. The control centres themselves don't undertake repairs, and are prevented from doing so by law.

6.22 Mushrooms

You may be used to seeing mushrooms sprout in your garden depending on the type of compost you used. If your new garden was in fact farmland or pasture at one point you may be surprised at the number and variety of fungi that grow at different times of the year. Obviously anything bright red or looking like something out of a fairy tale is best to be avoided but what about the others? Well you can by all accounts pick a selection of the ones you are unsure of and take them into your local pharmacy and they will advise as to which ones are safe [to eat] and which ones are not.

6.23 Newspapers

I said at the outset that I wasn't going to recommend or endorse products. One exception I will make is ConnexionFrance. As well as an informative website they issue a monthly English language newspaper in 'e' format or in actual print for 39€ for the year.

What they also produce that is very helpful are a series of guides about aspects of moving to and Life in France. I remembered this when my

So You're Thinking of Moving to France

'French Income Tax – What's new for 2018' arrived in the post as I started to draft this guide. They go through each form that you have to complete and explain how to fill it in. I used the comparable one last year and it was really helpful. Various French publications produce their own guides to but they obviously written in French, depends how good your language skills are?

Most regions have their own daily paper that covers local news and events and you will find a lot of useful information, papers, magazines and the like at the many regional airports in France.

6.23.1 Sports Newspapers

If you are a sports fan then you are well catered for in France with 2 sports specific newspapers of note.

a) L'Equipe

L'Equipe is a Paris based daily sports newspaper started shortly after the Second World War. It principally features Basketball, Cycling, Football, Formula 1, Rugby and Tennis although notionally will cover all sports.

b) Midi-Olympique

Midi Olympique is one of the oldest French Weekly newspapers, it was started in 1929, based in Toulouse, and is a bi-weekly newspaper on sale throughout the year that specialises in rugby. It is printed on distinctive coloured paper with the red edition available on Mondays which summarises and reports on the weekend matches. The green/weekend edition available on Fridays looks forward to the coming weekend matches and provides updates on team selections and injuries. As well as in depth coverage of the higher levels of French Rugby there is a small section on the English game and it covers Super Rugby, the Six Nations Tournament, The Rugby Championship and International fixtures.

6.24 Nuisance/Cold Calls

In addition to any features on your telephone handset if you start receiving nuisance/cold calls from companies that you do not have a professional relationship with you can register an account on Bloctel, a government run site (See Annex B) and enter the specific numbers to bar them.

So You're Thinking of Moving to France

6.25 Online Banking

We have become used to progressively more sophisticated online banking services over recent years, notably with the introduction of faster payments but things generally are much slower here in France.

6.25.1 Online Account

The clearing system is different to what you might expect in England and in particular online banking always seems to be 'missing' various debits when you look at your account as it takes longer for them to show up. This can be a source of great irritation when you look online and see your balance but then can't withdraw a lower level amount from the cash dispenser as what you can't see are the uncleared debits (and credits)

6.25.2 Banking Limits

Again you will likely have been used to making all manner of payments online. Two things to be aware of here are that your account will likely have a payment limit that will be lower than you expect so don't just assume because you have the money in your account that you can make a 5 figure transfer to a garage to buy a car for example. Equally once you have setup a new payee do not expect to be able to pay them instantly. It takes a further two days before any such payment is permissible.

6.26 Parcels from the UK

You will find that it is far cheaper to send yourself parcels from the UK than it is to send parcels back to the UK. So something to consider is that if you plan to travel back to the UK at regular intervals and are predisposed to check in additional suitcases on your low-cost flight ask yourself why when you can send yourself parcels of up to 29kg for far less than the cost of a suitcase. The only proviso being that the parcels can't contain anything with batteries otherwise it will be rejected at customs and returned to you at your expense. This gave me a problem when buying a new laptop (I bought English simply because I didn't want a French keyboard, as I had previous experience) as manufacturers will not ship them to France either, luckily my daughter came to the rescue by acting as courier on her next visit to see us.

So You're Thinking of Moving to France

6.27 Passport for ID

These days shopping for various items online has become part of our everyday life and many stores operate a 'click and collect' service. Be warned however, that strange as it seems when going to collect your purchases sometimes having an email print/on your phone and showing the credit card you bought it with is not enough. I took these things along to an electrical retailer shortly after we moved when I was trying to collect a new washing machine; we had sold our other one when we downsized, and I was told that was insufficient and they needed a passport. No amount of attempting to use logic, why would I have the printout and credit card it was ordered on if I wasn't me prevailed and I had to return the following day. Not all shops operate this policy but once bitten twice shy, if I haven't used a particular shop before I will take my passport with me as a precaution against a wasted journey.

6.28 Pollution Control

Some French cities and towns have introduced a requirement for an air quality sticker to be displayed on vehicle windscreens. The scheme is called 'Crit'Air' (*certificat qualité de l'air*) and is currently in the process of being introduced in many major cities. It means that some high-polluting vehicles may not be able to enter certain restricted areas during specific times.

There are six categories of sticker (each with unlimited duration) and these are colour-coded according to how much vehicles pollute and range from the cleanest (Crit'Air 1), for electric or hydrogen-powered vehicles, to the most polluting (Crit'Air 6).

There is no physical test involved, the classification is based on the age, size, and type of your vehicle and is determined by your registration number. See Annex B for more details.

6.29 Priorité à Droite

A nearby town has a very confusing mini roundabout as far as we are concerned as cars coming onto it have priority over those already on it. Although one is made aware of *Priorité à Droite* when one first drives in

So You're Thinking of Moving to France

France. There are no road signs here to indicate same and it seems the key to understanding this situation is to look for road markings. If there is no dotted line across your carriageway on the approach to the roundabout then you can indeed sail right onto it, however beware as at the next access point someone can do the same to you. Be cautious.

6.30   Pruning

You might think it strange to have a section on 'garden maintenance' in this guide but this pruning *Elagage* concerns maintenance of your boundary if it is adjacent to a main road as it is incumbent on property owners to maintain their hedges/trees particularly if they start to encroach on telephone wires or electricity cables.

In this part of the world too there has been concerns raised as the Departmental Council of Correze believes that pruning {trees and hedges] can increase the lifespan of the road network, especially by preventing falling leaves from rotting on the roadway. Their decision to install optical fibre overground (when it is underground in other *départements*) also contributes to this viewpoint. As a consequence some property owners including our neighbour have been served notices ordering them to prune relevant foliage otherwise the Departmental Council will arrange for the work to be done at the owners' expense.

Where the *département* has got involved directly it has left some areas of woodland seriously denuded and there has also been claims that owners have been overzealous in their housekeeping as a result. The simple message appears to be to prune your boundary on a regular basis.

6.31   Publicity Posters

Do not be surprised if on your travels you see out of date publicity for events. Sometimes the event in question can be weeks or months old, there seems to be no rush to remove them nor to place current posters on top of them to obscure them. In fact at Christmastime our local supermarket still had large posters next to the entrance for events that took place in July and August.

So You're Thinking of Moving to France

6.32   Roads

In July 2018 the law changed for safety reasons. The speed limit on any road without a central divider was reduced to 80kmh despite any signs still showing 90! The effectiveness of this change is due to be reviewed in the Summer of 2020 particularly as many *départements* were unhappy about the change in the first place.

6.33   Sans Contact

Over recent years contactless payments have become a boon as one can temporarily forget one's PIN number but still buy things. This is certainly true in France also with a transaction limit of 30€. However it seems that a lot of the EPOS systems here only allow such payments if you say so in advance as it seems the cashier needs to enter same on their till. Just dropping your card on the card reader can result in a payment refused message appearing on screen to your potential embarrassment, but is usually easily overcome if you then say you want to pay *Sans Contact*.

6.34   'Shed' Tax

Be careful if you plan to improve your outdoor space by installing e.g. a parking area, shed, solar panels (on the ground) or swimming pool as anything with a ground surface area more than 5m² will be subject to a *taxe d'aménagement*. This one-off tax is also levied on any construction or extension that needs a building permit.

It was introduced in 2012 and is aimed at assisting the funding of local work. A base rate is set each year and that is multiplied by the project's ground area and by the commune's total rate (usually between 1 & 5% but can reach 20% if large scale local work is being funded). There are some set rates, e.g. a pool is 200€ / m² whereas ground solar panels are 10€ / m² and some works are exempt. If the total amount is less than 1,500€ it is paid in full otherwise it is made in two payments in the 14th & 26th months after approval is granted.

6.35   Shutters

Want to install shutters on your house to give it a more authentic French look or want to change the colour of the existing ones? It's best to have a

So You're Thinking of Moving to France

word at the *Mairie* to make sure that you are not contravening anything in the local planning guidelines with regard to colour restrictions etc.

6.36   Slower Pace of Life

It is highly likely that a more relaxed and slower pace of life featured quite high on your list of reasons to move to France, so if you are impacted by it don't over-react. It is not uncommon to be standing behind someone in the Supermarket queue who then gets into an animated conversation with the cashier at the checkout. Both of them will seemingly be totally oblivious to the queue of waiting people and their, and your, growing impatience.

Equally you may be driving somewhere and encounter a delivery driver, other motorist or even postman blocking the road whilst talking to someone at the side of the road or in another vehicle. It will be obvious they have seen your vehicle draw up but will possibly be in no hurry to finish their discussion. The same applies if seeking assistance in a large store, the assistant may well see you standing there but will continue their sometimes lengthy conversation first or even when finished they will stop to answer the phone first before dealing with you. It will not be because you are English, it is just what they do. If this occurs just breathe in slowly and smile inwardly that you are no longer on the clock and have all the time in the world yourself.

6.37   Supermarkets & DIY Stores

6.37.1 Opening Hours

Supermarkets that open 24 hours a day do not exist in France, even in the big cities, and you are even pushed to find late-night opening. As a rule they will open around 8.30-9.00am and close between 7.00-7.30pm. Some, depending on location may even close at lunchtime. Again some will open for a time on Sundays, usually 09.00 and shut their doors between midday and 12.30pm although associated Petrol stations will stay open for credit/debit card payments only. Some supermarkets may even close slightly earlier in winter.

So You're Thinking of Moving to France

💡 Even DIY stores which you may be used to popping along to on a Sunday will shut their doors on a Saturday night until Monday morning.

6.37.2 Petrol

 Keep an eye out as those Super/Hypermarkets that have an associated Petrol Station usually (at least around the *Corrèze*) reduce their prices across all grades of 'petrol' at weekends.

6.37.3 Publicity

You will be surprised in the amount of publicity the supermarkets issue on a weekly basis. All the magazines containing current offers are usually delivered along with your post on Monday or Tuesday's, assuming you haven't blocked delivery of Junk Mail that is. (See section 6.17 above).

6.37.4 Offers

So you have spotted an offer in the magazine, gone along to the supermarket, found it in stock and taken in to the till along with the rest of your shopping only to find that when you get back home that your receipt shows a totally different price. I have to say that this not uncommon as there seems to be frequent disconnects between the magazines, the shelf-edge labels and the EPOS system at the till. So if you are buying something that you expect to be on offer either watch the price as it is scanned or check your receipt before you leave the store. It really is really a case of Caveat Emptor.

That said, if I only spot something when I get home I query it next time I am in store and have not once been refused a refund.

6.38   Swimming Pools and Alarms

So having lived in 'the One' for a period and experienced the climate here you may think that installing an inground or ground level swimming pool will be a good idea? However, due to the high rate of infant mortality by drowning in pools, France has some of the most stringent rules regarding the building of new swimming pools and consequently they need to be equipped with one of the following standard safety devices.

So You're Thinking of Moving to France

These can be either be a [usually transparent] shelter that one retracts before using the pool although high ones allow one to still swim in poor weather, but sometimes these shelters cost more to install than the actual pool itself. An alarm that activates when it detects entry of a certain weight or more to the water, a pool cover for when the pool is not in use, or a barrier or gated fence surround. Use of these last two measures in combination is quite common.

The rules apply for both paying guests, at your *Gite* or B&B for instance, and your family.

6.39   Taxes

As the owner of a French property you will become familiar with 3 principal taxes.

6.39.1 Income Tax

Over the years we have all become familiar with the HMRC Self-Assessment process with tax returns having to be completed by September or the following January for the tax year ending the previous April 5th. The French system is a little different, it is based on a Tax Household *Foyer Fiscal* and the number of people within it. The French tax year equates to the calendar year and returns have to be completed in the following May. The actual date within May varies depending on your *Département* number, the lower the earlier.

Until 2019 income tax was payable annually in arrears but this year saw the introduction of *prélèvement à la source* (PAS), basically a PAYE system for those in employment, and retirees were also included with monthly payments due based on $1/_{12}$ the previous year's tax payable. Despite this everyone still has to make an annual declaration and everyone has to complete a French Tax return, including if one gets income from letting a property in France irrespective of where one lives. **Remember, the country that one pays tax in is defined in law and is not a matter of personal choice!**

N.b. As an individual you are responsible for making the declaration, **non receipt of relevant forms is not acceptable as an excuse.**

So You're Thinking of Moving to France

As a first timer you will need to fill in and send off paper forms that one can download from the Government Tax website (See Annex B). As a minimum you will likely need the following forms *formulaires* and accompanying notes:

    2042   - Formulaire principal
    2042C - Revenu complémentaire
    2047   - Revenus de l'étranger
    3916   - Comptes de déclaration tenus à l'étranger?

Thereafter you can setup an online tax account and make subsequent submissions electronically. Your tax bill is then calculated by the Tax Office and you are notified of the amount owing during the summer. If you are due a refund it will be paid in September, if you need to pay more then any amount under 300€ is payable then, else the difference is split over the 4 remaining months of the year.

There are numerous guides available for one to purchase that can help you with your submission but these are generally published before the Tax Authorities finalise their forms (as like HMRC they constantly tweak them year on year) and so they refer to last year's forms. If you are unsure you can always engage the services of an accountant.

6.39.2 Taxe D'habitation

Taxe D'habitation is like Council Tax in the UK. It is either payable by the person who is residing in the property on the 1st January each year or the owner by default. The tax is generally payable in October/November of that year though your *Notaire* may make the necessary payment on your behalf as part of the purchase process. The monies raised by this tax go to your commune who set the rate to be paid but it is based on the Cadastral Rental value of the house and its' outbuildings There are reductions/exemptions for households with lower incomes.

6.39.3 Taxe Foncière

Taxe Foncière can be viewed as a land and building ownership tax and is paid by whoever owns the property on 1st January each year and is based on a notional rental value as adjusted by the age, size and condition of the property. This money too goes to the commune, who set the rate, and amongst other things covers the cost of rubbish collection. This tax is

So You're Thinking of Moving to France

generally paid in October/November although when you purchase a property the tax for the year is generally paid pro-rata by the Vendor and Purchaser and sorted out by the *Notaire(s)*.

6.40   TV Licence Fee

There is a TV licence fee payable in France but as with other things there is an exemption for those on a low income. It is called simply the fee *la redevance* and is a *contribution à l'audiovisuel public* which funds the five public television channels in mainland France - France 2, France 3, France 4, France 5, and Arte.

The fee is revised annually and collected each November/December with the annual tax demand for the *taxe d'habitation*, (See section 6.37.2) where it will be listed separately.

6.41   Ticks

Part of the spider family, these parasitic insects satisfy all of their nutritional needs by feeding on a diet of blood. They are perhaps best known for transmission of Lyme disease to humans although not all their bites are harmful. You can't escape these insidious parasites in France and if you or your dog(s) move through any grassy areas and/or woodland then you are at a higher risk of tick bites, especially between April through September when they are most active. If you have a large amount of grass with 'the One' then you need to carefully inspect your dogs on a regular basis or after you have walked them. That said we cannot always see them on Keno and he is all white!

If you find that they do have ticks attached you can simply remove them by pressing down on them with your finger and then turning it anti-clockwise up to a dozen times or by twisting them out with Tick Hooks which you can obtain online or from your local vets. Not all dogs are happy with you doing this so alternatively you can take the precautionary route and use Tick collars or obtain Tick tablets for your pets from the vets. The latter are available for periods of one or three months during which they provide them with some resistance to the effects of tick bites.

So You're Thinking of Moving to France

6.42   Water Storage

Finding 'the One' with lots of land and flowers, plants, shrubs and vegetables is one thing, keeping it looking presentable is another, especially in the summer when temperatures can easily exceed 40°C in the southern parts of the country. For that you need water and lots of it, and that means some form of storage solution. Sure there are always hosepipes, but unless you have access to a Well then you are likely to be on a water meter and nothing will set the dial spinning more than turning the hose on each day.

Consequently acquiring containers to store water in is a necessity. If you have any and they are reasonably clean you can use old oil drums else you will need to purchase some purpose built Water Butts from your local *Brico* but you will also then need to buy a connector kit, cover, stand and tap which are all sold separately and the cost then starts to mount up. Instead wait for your local supermarket to run a promotion or *déstockage* event where you can pick up a complete ensemble far cheaper!

The types of Butts sold generally range in size from 200 to 500 litres or 1,000 litres but as an alternative, and this depends very much on your budget, you could utilise a plastic *Fosse Septique* tank placed above ground which will give you in excess of 3,000 litre capacity (bear in mind that the average UK bath holds c67 litres) however if you go down this route you will likely need a submersible pump with an appropriate hose fitting to be able to extract and utilise the contents. By appropriate I mean a 'semi-rigid' hosepipe rather than one of the 'lay flat' variety as these are prone to bending over at right angles when they exit the butt and restricting the flow.

We inherited some such storage and have acquired additional capacity, since, as such we have some 8,500 litres available for the produce in our vegetable patch and polytunnel which provides some 3-4 weeks supply should we need it during the really hot weather.

So You're Thinking of Moving to France

6.43   Websites.

As a society we have become used to buying goods or tickets or looking up information via a search engine or a company's website. However here in France your digital experience may not be what you are used to. I have already remarked that it is common to see posters (See section 6.28) advertising things that are long since out of date but the same is sometimes also true of company websites as their content management in general is woefully lacking by UK standards.

Even comparatively simple things like the display of opening and closing hours cannot always be believed. If you have not been to a particular store before then do not plan to go just as it opens or just before closing as you may well be disappointed! Give yourself some additional time.

Many companies that have websites just use them for display purposes with no link to a purchasing function. Equally the in-site search facilities don't always return every product they sell and you will not always find the latest result or match report on sports clubs site's for example.

In connection with this our instant society expects that if we contact a supplier through their website that they respond to our question/complaint within a matter of hours, this does not seem to be the case here and you can easily wait days for a response. I had a problem with a brushcutter that had come apart so I emailed the manufacturers support desk and although I got an automatically generated support ticket number it took them 10 days to reply to my mail. In the meantime I had got fed up with the wait and taken it back to the store.

A word of warning about filling in your details if making an order on a French website. Many of them make it mandatory to enter a French mobile telephone number, rather than a landline number. Curiously this situation applies when trying to setup ones *DMP Dossier Médical Partage* which enables one to keep all one's health information online and share it with the health professionals of your choice.

So You're Thinking of Moving to France

Of course their sites' validation doesn't always tell you this you have to work it out. So if you don't have one enter a friends number if you can or otherwise create a dummy one such as 0600000011 to enable you to move on and complete the purchase.

6.44   Winter Truce

La trêve hivernale or the so called winter truce runs for five months from November 1st until midnight on 31st March and marks a period when French landlords are not legally allowed to forcibly evict their tenants **for any reason**. The truce is meant as a humanitarian gesture, to ensure that people (but not squatters) do not end up homeless in the coldest part of the year. During this period it is also illegal for landlords to cut off gas and electricity supplies in the event of unpaid bills.

However, a landlord can begin proceedings during the winter truce to look to evict any tenants who do not pay their rent, or who refuse to leave after being given the contractual notice period. However, this still requires a court order from a judge at the local *tribunal d'instance*, which the tenants can appeal.

Once any final judgment is made then the landlord has to give the eviction order via a bailiff, and the tenant then has, depending on the judgment, at least two months to leave, though it can't take place during *La trêve hivernale*.

6.45   Woodburning Stoves

If 'the One' has a woodburning stove(s) you will obviously need to source a supply of wood to use through the winter. This may come from trees on your own land although received wisdom is that anything cut 'this year' should be allowed to dry out for a year before using the next. Alternatively you can buy *Bois de Chauffage* from a commercial source.

Only experience, or information received from your Vendor, will tell how much wood you need on average each year but what quantities of measure do you buy it in?

- A stère (a term which originates from the original metric system) equates to a cubic metre of wood – usually in 1 metre lengths.

So You're Thinking of Moving to France

- A cord is approximately 3½ stères although it depends on the size of the pieces and the airspace between them.

The price you are generally quoted is for 1 metre lengths but do not make the mistake of thinking you can easily cut it to size (say 50cm lengths) just before you need it as even if you use a chainsaw it will take you much longer than you think. Believe me it is far simpler to ask the merchant to cut it to the length you want, before delivery and pay the 20-30€ extra!

6.46 Your Address

Obviously you know where you live and can describe it to family/friends who visit easily enough but it is not always obvious to delivery drivers, particularly if you are just known by a house name and a commune.

Consequently I suggest that if you have accounts on say Amazon or Ebay, any other supplier that you make regular purchases from or just when making adhoc orders that you change the first line of your address in your profile to include your specific GPS Co-ordinates, something in the format of

<House Name> (GPS nn.nnnnnn, n.nnnnnn)
<Road>
<Commune>

etc. then there should be no excuse for not getting deliveries to your front door.

Because a lot of courier companies still give an expected delivery timeslot of between 0800 and 1800 they give one the opportunity to have one's parcels delivered to a nearby collection point, e.g. a *Bibliothèque*, or *Tabac* so if there is something that needs a signature, is valuable, or you are just going to be out for the day then take advantage of this facility.

That said it would seem that not all companies use satellite navigation as on one expected delivery I received an email saying that they couldn't find my address and needed explicit instructions. Incredulous I know and clearly their schedule did not allow time to stop at the *Mairie* to find ou where the house was. I did state in my reply that it was impossible to be

So You're Thinking of Moving to France

more explicit than GPS Co-ordinates and also referred to the competence of the driver but rather than set off on a long rant I just sent them directions from the Supermarket in town. The parcel arrived the next day!

So You're Thinking of Moving to France

7. Boys Toys

7.1 Introduction

In this section I am not talking about the tools one might regularly see in a toolbox such as hammers, pliers, saws, screwdrivers etc. Or even the ancillary items that one accumulates such as a Circular Saw, Drill, or Sander or depending on your property say a Post Rammer or Winch. No the kind of thing I am talking about is the type of kit that one doesn't necessarily need back in the UK with much smaller gardens to tend. These may seem like an extravagance, particularly if one's budget is tight but they will more than pay for themselves in a relatively short time period by saving you time and effort and you will soon become proficient in a range of skills you didn't know you had. I am not suggesting that you go out and buy them all at once, it should be needs based and you can always borrow from friends in the first instance to inform your decision.

7.2 Battery, Electric or Petrol

Once you have decided on what tool you need the first question you have to ask yourself is what type of tool do I buy, Battery, Electric or Petrol and when I say Petrol this encompasses Diesel? For the larger than average grounds of a French property I would suggest that you want to strongly consider a Petrol powered device, although that does mean you will likely be spending more on them.

7.2.1 Battery Powered

Of course you can consider battery powered devices and believe me where there is a need you can find a device, I was amazed!. Consequently you will not be surprised to find that battery powered All in One's, Chainsaw's, Hedge Cutters, Mower's and Strimmer's etc all exist. I have personally never contemplated such a machine on our plot due to its sheer size but if you are thinking battery powered then I guess the type of questions you need to ask yourself are:

- How long does a battery last (from which you can determine how much work you will get done on a single charge)?
- How long does a battery take to charge?
- How much does a [spare] battery cost?

So You're Thinking of Moving to France

- Are there different rated batteries (power) for each tool?

As I am thinking you need at least two per tool, one on while you are working and one charging. In which case a further question then arises:
- Are the batteries interchangeable (between devices)?
  (It is possible that even tools from the same manufacturer will have different fittings in which case that will be more outlay).

What you don't want to happen is to start a job and have to continually stop some way through it to wait for the battery/spare to charge.

7.2.2 Electric Powered
So it may be that you discount battery powered devices for all but the smallest jobs and go with Electrical as that is probably what you have been used to in the UK.

But you have to think practically, how far is it from your front door/back door and the nearest socket to the edge of your boundary? It is not just a case of whether you have an extension lead long enough or even multiple leads and a circuit breaker you can use but can you realistically see yourself outside using your electrical appliances? For one thing wet or even damp weather can greatly restrict your usage and secondly you need to think of the Electricity consumption if you are spending hours using them. Electricity in France is not cheap.

7.2.3 Petrol Powered
So for these reasons allied to the size of our plot and the distances involved my personal preference is to opt for petrol powered tools.

I will now attempt a brief discussion on the type of Petrol toys you might need. The majority of them require a different mix of Petrol and 2 Stroke Oil to run. Consequently I suggest you label up separate bottles with an indelible pen to store the different mixtures in. They won't perform well, if at all, with the wrong mixture.

The one thing you will not find in this list is a strimmer. Reason being is that I have had a few but irrespective of the make and the care one takes with them I have found that after a while this concept of a command

So You're Thinking of Moving to France

feed just doesn't work. Whether it is by pressing a button or banging the spool they all jam and to me seem a complete waste of time and money.

7.3   All in 1

You know the kind of thing I mean. Where there is a base power unit and you plug in/on various attachments, extensions and handles. I started off with a 4 in 1 brushcutter, hedge trimmer, pruner, and strimmer. To start with you only tend to use a couple of the attachments far more than the others so you are paying for things you don't really need. I also tended to use the pruner as a substitute chainsaw which it really isn't. But secondly and more importantly I would argue that they cannot necessarily be a master of all trades and that with continual mixed use they will wear out far quicker than a purpose built tool. Mine did after a year, caught fire in fact!

7.4   Brushcutter

A *Débroussailleuse* is basically a long pole with a triangular/solid metal disc on the end that spins around at high speed. It is therefore more robust and can cut through thicker vegetation than a strimmer and are my preference in this department. They come with both motors & blades of differing sizes so you 'pays your money and takes your choice' depending on the work you have planned for it. They are ideal for cutting a path through brambles or cutting down grass under low hanging tree branches where you might not be able to reach with your mower. A purpose built one will come with a harness that you strap on and helps you bear the weight.

Through experience when using a brushcutter I would always use a helmet with safety visor or safety goggles as a minimum and leather work gloves as if you inadvertently flick up a stone it will travel at high speed, and hurt!

So You're Thinking of Moving to France

7.5 Chainsaw

The *Tronçonneuse* is an extremely useful adjunct to one's toolbox indeed I would say that having one is fundamental to your new life here.

 However they are not to be taken lightly as Chainsaws do not take any prisoners. Other tools in your armoury may cut/bruise you if they are mishandled, but any accident with a chainsaw is likely to be serious and involve a rapid trip to the hospital.

Extreme care should be taken when using your Chainsaw but these are ideal for taking the hard work out of pruning thick hedges, cutting down trees or the ivy from them or making logs for your woodburner They have a tendency to stick in the item you are cutting if you don't observe some basic laws of physics, and you have to be careful trying to extract them else you can damage the bar and/or the chain and need replacements.

 Only buy a longer length saw (more than 12") once you are accomplished using one of the smaller versions.

It is good practice, some will say a necessity, to at least wear some safety gear when using your chainsaw. Some or all of a helmet with safety visor and/or ear defenders, leather work gloves, boots or shoes with 'toe tectors' and even Chainsaw Protective trousers which have multiple abrasive resistant layers should be considered, avoid loose clothing too.

Also through experience when out cutting trees I will take along a bowsaw and a crowbar in case the chainsaw gets stuck and you need to free the blade quickly without incurring any damage.

7.6 Crowbar

A Crowbar *pince à levier* is not usually thought of in terms of boys toys but for me it is an ideal piece of kit, providing it is 4 ft /120cm long! The type I am talking about has one flat/slightly curved end and one very curved end with a hammer like claw feature. I originally bought mine to assist in dismantling the old decking as the leverage it is capable of exerting using either end will remove even the most stubborn screw.

So You're Thinking of Moving to France

But since then it has proved to be a great tool in the garden and on the drive as our land is extremely rocky once you get say 6" down. You'll know what I mean if you have ever bent a garden fork(s) whilst digging out holes. Trying to remove a large piece of rock or stone just isn't easy with a fork unless you dig a far bigger hole than you need. Using the crowbar makes life far simpler, use the flat end to find the edge of the rock, work your way down the side and then lever it out, works every time. The crowbar is also good for digging post holes, prising off ancient ivy or helping to remove Metposts or tree stumps with the right fulcrum.

7.7 Generator

Living in the countryside a Generator *Groupe électrogène* really comes into its own as power cuts are a way of life unfortunately, and not just in the winter. Our worst one was on the 4th July (yes really) 2018 when a huge storm crossed the country taking out fences, power lines, roof tiles etc. We lost power at 1800 on the Wednesday and it wasn't restored until around 1330 on the Saturday. I was lucky as I had a pre-booked trip back to the UK from the Thursday to Sunday so Joanne bore the brunt of it with candles in the house and going out in the car to charge her phone and Ipad etc. but the compensation we received from EDF a few months later was scant consolation for the annoyance caused.

This was the third such occasion we had lost power for some time (once while we were away on holiday), so I decided that we had lost enough freezer food and that we needed a generator. They come in all shapes, sizes and prices and there are plenty of online calculators available to help determine the one that meets your requirements. I was not thinking about something that would power the whole house necessarily just keeping the essentials going like fridges and freezers and being able to make cups of tea or coffee. It doesn't need to automatically start when the power fails as I am happy to go and fire it up as required. A friend has a 3kw machine but when it is running it trips out if he switches the kettle or TV on which seems onerous so I went for a 5kw version which gives us a bit more flexibility. We can run the fridges and freezers, have some lights on and make tea without worrying about having to restart it.

So You're Thinking of Moving to France

Because of the radial circuitry in French houses you need to be careful plugging the generator into your domestic supply. **You must ensure your main input circuit breaker/isolation switch is set to OFF**, then start your generator and simply plug it into a standard power socket to power your house. **But be sure to stop and disconnect your generator first prior to re-setting the breaker when you finish using it.**

Different generators have varying sizes of petrol tank and this combined with their hourly petrol consumption gives differing periods of autonomy. In the case of an extended power outage it becomes a matter of personal choice and practicality as to how long you run them for. Consider for example whether you need to run your generator on a 24 hour basis or just during waking hours as freezers will happily go through the night without power with minimal impact on their contents providing the door remains closed? The reason being that some generators use upwards of 25-30 ltr for c11 hours electricity production so the costs for running them for a day start to mount up and could easily begin to outweigh the costs of any food you are trying to save but clearly come into their own if enabling heating systems to carry on running.

7.8   Hedge Trimmers

A *taille-haie* is essential if like us you have almost 200m or more of hedging boundary that needs upkeep. It would lead to severe cases of RSI (Repetitive Strain Injury) if you had to cut this amount by hand, so having powered assistance is essential. Anything thicker than the hedge trimmer can manage can easily be dealt with by your chainsaw.

7.9   Mower

The typical plot size here renders your average Flymo redundant and you just need some form of powered *Tondeuse*. The standard kind that you walk behind and push is adequate depending on the type of terrain and its size but for most of the larger properties you will need to consider a [*Tondeuse*] *autoportée* or ride on mower.

Our plot is over 2 hectares and when you discount the Barn, Drive, *Etang*, House, Woods and boundary area I reckon there is almost 4 acres that needs regular mowing.

So You're Thinking of Moving to France

The garden which was pasture in a previous life slopes every which way and the ground is prone to moles *taupes* and their holes. I spoke with a couple of local garden supply shops who were very helpful and offered to come and size up my garden and recommend the right piece of hardware but the tractors and machinery there were proposing were too rich for my blood. I was also apprehensive as I never previously owned a house that required me to use one before. A chance conversation with a friend at a quiz night helped me enormously. He had 9 acres, with slopes and mole holes and said that his ride-on was more than a match for the job. I then rang a company in England and spoke to a salesman for 40 minutes about the merits of different models and pretty much made my decision based on that. I went to see him when I was next in the country, tried it out with a test drive and then arranged to buy it and have it shipped over as a part load. (See section 4.5). Talking to the salesman had another advantage, he offered to fit a 50mm ball hitch to the back of the mower before I took delivery so I could use it to pull a trailer if I needed/wanted to. Without it I would need a trailer with a universal hitch pin attachment

> N.b I know that earlier in this guide I have advocated shopping locally but I was far happier having a detailed and technical conversation in my native language. However when we bought our car I was happy to do that from a French dealership.

In the end I went for the next model up in the range than my friend had, as well as a slightly bigger engine and better suspension it had a 120cm cutting deck not 102cm. Not much difference you might think but if your garden is say 100m long isn't it better to make a minimum of 83 passes across to cut it (dependent on contours and the position of ponds and trees etc) rather than 98? Then factor in mowing every couple of weeks between say April and September and that is a lot of time saved.

13 June 2019

So You're Thinking of Moving to France

7.9.1   Type of Mower

I said at the outset that I would not get involved in technical challenges so whether you need a simple ride-on, zero turn model or lawn tractor you will have to determine yourself, as I did. I never had the need for such a mower before and found the potential choice a little daunting, until the conversation with my friend. Choose wisely because you will find that a decent ride-on will likely cost as much as any second-hand car you may have bought.

Once you have homed in on your type and make you then need to decide whether you are mowing and collecting the grass or mowing and mulching it? As far as I was concerned it was a 'no-brainer'. Given the size of our plot compared with the average size collector box on the back of a mower I foresaw endless trips back up the garden to an ever growing compost pile to empty the container and so steered well away from those models.

View a mulching mower as like a large scale cross-cut paper shredder as it goes about its business, consequently my mower mulches the grass and spits it out laterally for it to be broken down by sun, wind and rain rather than gather it up in a collector box.

A word of warning, don't be tempted to buy a mower from your local hypermarket. Yes, some of their prices are extremely attractive but they are not going to service it for you or repair it if it goes wrong. Whereas if you go for a well-known brand it is far simpler to find a service centre.

So You're Thinking of Moving to France

7.9.2 Advantages of Mulching

Any gardener will tell you that if you mulch your grass it is good for your lawn. The reason being that the quickly decomposing cuttings provide free, essential and natural organic nutrients because as they break down, the cuttings will release nitrogen, potash and phosphate etc. Scientists will also tell you that you will find smaller quantities of calcium, iron, and magnesium that your lawn needs to stay healthy as worms help carry these nutrients back into the earth. What is more this is as good as any commercial fertiliser you might buy and what is even better, it is free.

Contrast this to depositing your collector contents into a compost heap which may well attract different types of vermin, or if you start bagging it up you will have numerous costly trips to the *déchetterie* to make.

7.9.3 Basic Precautions/Maintenance

With the cost of even a second-hand ride on likely running to 4 figures I suggest you need to take some basic precautions both before and after using it.

- Follow the manufacturers service schedule, even if you do it yourself;
- Carry out monthly maintenance checks/ top up the grease points, the most important generally being the front axle and on each spindle housing on the cutting deck to maintain grease from the top pulleys to the blades. It also ensures the cavity within the housing is dry;
- Prior to going out each time pat down all the molehills as any stones/ rocks they contain could damage your cutting blades;
- Pick up any large sticks/pieces of wood as they too can damage the blades, a particular problem for us Alfie loves chasing sticks when thrown or just taking one off chewing it and leaving the residue wherever he fancies, so we encourage him to return them;
- When out on the mower for any length of time wear ear protection and if prone to hay fever wear a mask too;
- Whilst mowing I try to ensure that I put the front tyre through any molehills that I might have missed as apart from flattening them you can also easily see if they contain any rocks; and
- Brush or vacuum off any residual grass cuttings when you have finished before putting the mower back in the garage.

So You're Thinking of Moving to France

7.9.4   Flat Tyres

I find mowing quite therapeutic; I use the 2 hours it takes to plan out any jobs that I have to undertake or think about trips I would like to make. On one occasion I was blissfully away scuba-diving in the Maldives whilst trying to create a path through the long grass between our pond and *étang* but the mower slipped down a small bank and got stuck. I had to walk back up the garden and seek Joanne's help to come and sit on it and engage reverse whilst I lifted the front bumper and applied serious grunt to shift it back on track. That done I drove it back to the barn only to find that the wheel that had gone down the bank had a puncture. Rather than get into the difficult task of trying to remove it, take it to a garage and 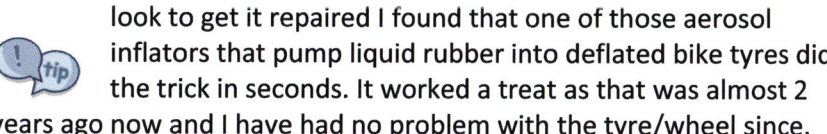 look to get it repaired I found that one of those aerosol inflators that pump liquid rubber into deflated bike tyres did the trick in seconds. It worked a treat as that was almost 2 years ago now and I have had no problem with the tyre/wheel since.

7.9.5   Add Ons – Chain Harrow

If you have a large amount of land or even a meadow it is unlikely you will get it to lawn standard. My machine has 12 different depths of cut from 1-4" and I never go below 2½". However, providing that you have a reasonably powered mower, say >15Hp you could fit a Chain Harrow. This is best described as an interlinking set of chains that look akin to the springs on an old style bed, the difference being they have a set of spikes pointing downwards that dig into and scour the soil. These are flexible enough to follow the ground contours can penetrate grass in even the toughest pasture. They help remove dead vegetation from lawns, paddocks and large grassed areas and are also suitable for preparing seed beds and levelling them.

7.9.6   Add Ons – Trailer

If you have a 'garden' big enough to warrant acquiring a ride-on mower then chances are you will need a trailer attachment of some description as well. I knew that I would benefit from one, to collect cut up logs from the woods or soil from molehills, to move waste to the bonfire area etc. You need to choose carefully as there will be a weight restriction as to what your mower can safely pull. I was advised not to exceed 500kg in

So You're Thinking of Moving to France

total on level ground and you still have to consider the "drag" factor, such as slopes (of which I have plenty), ground conditions and ground cover etc. To be on the safe side I factored in my weight and the weight of the trailer itself in my calculations of likely load capacity.

I figured that my general use car trailer was too big and heavy so needed something smaller and more specific. I eschewed a 'tipping' type trailer which people usually recommend for gardens as a lot of them are of plastic construction and I couldn't find anything suitable at a reasonable price as I didn't want a type that you have to put together yourself. In the end I opted for a small, light single axle car trailer weighing only 63kg that can be loaded with 337 kg (0.386 m^3). Although these trailers can be more problematic. They can tend to be too heavy and the draw bars too high and the recommendation is usually for a lawn tractor trailer but my small trailer works a treat on my terrain and I don't have to worry about the electric connections.

7.10   Quad Bike

With a *Quad* we really are talking boys toys but if you can justify one to yourself then all well and good. I thought short and hard about acquiring one but once the novelty wore off I wondered what I would use it for? Assuming it was road legal I could use it to go to the local supermarket if I wanted as it is only 1½ miles away but how quickly would I get bored of just riding it around the garden? If you don't have a ride-on mower I can see a case for it if you equip it so that you can attach a small trailer, then it will help you in and around the garden, otherwise it is just pure indulgence, isn't it?

So You're Thinking of Moving to France

7.11   Towbar

Not exactly a toy more of a necessity if you live in this part of the world. I know it is expensive to have one fitted to your car if you don't already have one, but nevertheless it is essential to be able to pull a caravan, horse box or trailer either using a fixed or detachable towbar. The other consideration for you is your choice of electrical connection it has. If you are going out of your way to have one fitted then a 13 pin plug will give you maximum flexibility when towing and you will usually get a 7 pin-13 pin converter given to you as part of the installation

7.12   Trailers

Along with a Chainsaw I would say that a *Remorque* is the most essential toy you will need. Believe me you will be surprised. From removal of excess garden waste, clearing out old barns and removing the contents to the *Déchetterie* to collecting assorted materials from the Builders Merchant or *Brico* store your trailer will soon become indispensable. I initially thought about hiring one when I needed it but having used mine on average 3 times a month or more since I have been here it has soon paid for itself. I was lucky in that shortly before we moved here a Hypermarket opened nearby and they had a very good promotional deal available which swayed me.

In terms of what to look out/obtain for I would strongly suggest you get a trailer with twin axles rather than a single. Not only is it more stable but using a jockey wheel at the front of the tongue near the hitch or coupler is something of a pfaff methinks.

My trailer came with detachable extra height side panels (but I opt not to fit these as it places extra strain on the back when trying to lift things out) and also a cover/tarpaulin *bâche*.

Trailers come with their own 'road documentation' – details of the weight they can legally carry etc. It is therefore best to keep this in your car as you need to be able to produce it if the trailer is attached and you are stopped by the authorities.

So You're Thinking of Moving to France

7.13   Wood Chipper

If you have or anticipate a lot of garden waste of the woody variety then a *Déchiqueteuse* or *Broyeur de Végétaux* is a good idea. The principal drawback is that petrol ones are very expensive, think 4 figures for a moderate sized one. This leads one to an immediate dilemma. How do you know that the specific model will do the job you want it to and you haven't wasted your money? Particularly as in the past I have found that the stated thickness of wood that it will shred can be a bit of an exaggeration. I explained the dilemma to my local *Motoculture* – Garden Equipment man and he was very understanding. We worked out prices for hiring for a day and also for a weekend, that way I could see whether the large scale investment would be worth it and whether I would have enough demand too. After all there are only so many paths you can create or weed suppressant you can use.

Ideally whatever machine you opt for needs to have a reversible mode, you don't want to try and prise any jammed log out of it and the difficulties that brings, a bit like paper jammed in your shredder but on a more industrial scale.

So You're Thinking of Moving to France

8. Domestic Gadgets

I was originally going to call this section Girls Gadgets, not because I am sexist but just because I like alliteration in sentences, however I didn't want to give the PC brigade an excuse to complain, so I played it safe.

That said some of the following may be stereotypical in that the gadgets are food oriented. I can't help it, my girlie is the sort that will look in the fridge 5 minutes after I have said 'we need to go shopping' and concoct a stunning 2 course meal. Consequently the things that float her boat are mainly in the edible department. So the following things may prove useful.

8.1   Apple Peeler

We live surrounded by orchards and indeed have a few apple trees of our own, the difference being that ours have no chemicals used on them. However even our small number of trees produce far more apples than we can eat at any one time, and that is after taking some down to the staff at the *Mairie* or giving them to friends.

The choice therefore is to throw the excess away/let them rot or to try and store them for cooking at a later point. Consequently a simple Apple Peeler *Pèle Pommes* helps prepare them for this. It looks like a spiraliser and is just a giant corkscrew on which you mount the apple and a spring blade which removes the skin as you turn it. Using it makes light work of peeling and you can do dozens in a fraction of the time it would take manually, our grandson loves it. The apples are then in an ideal state to cook and puree before freezing.

8.2   Apple Steamer

Still on the subject of apples, a *Vapeur Pommes* is just a simple three tier steamer. Cram the apples into the top, put water into the bottom and boil for about an hour. The steam rises and the juice is extracted from the apples and falls into the middle container where it can be siphoned off.

So You're Thinking of Moving to France

8.3   Automatic Watering System

The additional land that comes with many French houses compared with the UK means that one doesn't need to consider taking an allotment as there is usually more than enough space to create your own vegetable patch and the better climate means that you can consider growing a wide variety of produce.

Once planted though it needs constant tending if it is not to go to waste. During the long hot summers this means regular watering so what better than to install a *Système d'arrosage automatique* or Automatic Watering System. Utilising timers and with hoses linked to a water source, an external tap or water butt, the system will switch on/off at designated times of the day and run for pre-determined lengths of time to deliver water to your plants or vegetables.

8.4   Electric Bicycle

I have to state up front that we don't possess a *Vélo à assistance électrique* but when I asked the memsahib what sort of things would improve her life here this is what she chose. Although some of them have prices that would make your eyes water like most technological items their price will lower over time.

Taking their power from on-board batteries these 'e-bikes' assist your pedalling efforts and do a lot of your work for you meaning you can be more relaxed whether you have a type that is designed for the road or a mountain type model. There are some fairly steep hills near about and I am sure she had visions of going to the local boulangerie on a road bike and pedalling back with her wares in a little basket on the front. Still, if your budget runs to it why not?

8.5   Polytunnel

These semi-circular tunnels made from hoops of steel and covered in polythene are extremely popular here. Placed in sunny spots they work on basic physics in that the inside heats up faster than the hot air can escape the structure and thus they help provide a fertile environment for your plants or vegetables. You still have to tend and water them but the

So You're Thinking of Moving to France

extra heat stimulates growth and also protects them from any bad weather.

Just a cautionary note, in high summer it can get very hot inside, too hot in fact and it is best to leave the door and window(s) open during the day otherwise the contents can easily die off.

8.6   Rotavator

In keeping with the theme of vegetable patches and Polytunnels digging them over can be backbreaking work so mechanical assistance is desirable. Thus a *Motobineuse thermique* or Rotavator is ideal, and as with the many 'Boys Toys' (See section 7) the most practical is a petrol powered device, particularly as any such patch/tunnel is likely to be some distance from the house.

These machines have a series of rotating blades which enable the soil to be easily broken up and turned over and in so doing they aerate the soil. This in turn improves drainage of the area and makes it more receptive to growing your chosen plants or crops.

8.7   Staple Gun

I don't mean the kind of Staple Gun *Agrafeuse* that you use for building jobs and the like but the smaller electric kind that one would use for craft type projects and that 'fire' staples or tacks. Not only are they extremely handy for securing upholstery to furniture like Chairs or Headboards which you may already own or may have picked up from a Flea Market *Brocante*, but they do come into their own outside the house as well when for example lining *Potager* or Plant Boxes with sheeting before filling them with earth/compost, for which they are really indispensable.

If you are renovating a house or getting ready to open a *Chambres d'hôte* then I figure you will have a lot of this type of work to do, so go get one.

Questions for Estate Agents

Annex A

Here are the questions that worked for us when we asked, modify it according to the features of the property you are enquiring about.

1) When did the property go on the market?
2) What position are the owners in?
3) Can we have a floor plan - hand drawn is ok (and it doesn't have to be to scale) so we can see if the layout works for us?
4) Do you have any aerial view or plan cadastral (with *parcelle* no.s) if possible?
5) What type of heating system is used?
6) Is there underfloor heating?
7) Is there double glazing?
8) Is there ADSL already at the property?
9) Do you have any other pictures than those posted on the advert?
10) An indication of the location, is it on a main/village road etc?
11) Is there any commerce in the nearest village?
12) Is the land around the house fenced, if not how is it delineated
13) Does the septic tank conform to the 2012 regulations?
14) How much is the *Taxe Fonciere*?
15) How much is the *Taxe D'habitation*?
16) What size is the swimming pool?
17) Is it fresh/salt water before being chlorinated?
18) Is it covered?
19) Is it heated?
20) Is it alarmed?
21) Is it fenced?
22) Is the *Gite* currently let out and if so during what period?
23) What income is generated from this?
24) Is there a separate website for advertising the *Gite*?
25) If so is it included in the sale?
26) Do the outbuildings have light, power and water installed?

13 June 2019   Annex A

Useful Addresses

Annex B

I have mainly shown the web addresses of sites you may find useful until you source your own favourites, I have deliberately not included any Banks or Insurance Companies as I don't want it alleged that I am giving financial advice, nor Estate Agents as they tend to be regional in focus although I have included a well-known 'E-Agency'.

Animal Adoption

30 Million Friends	https://www.30millionsdamis.fr/jagis/jadopte-un-animal/
Orfee	http://association-orfee.forumactif.com/f7-les-chiens-d-orfee-a-adopter
Second Chance	https://www.secondechance.org/
SPA	https://www.la-spa.fr/adopter-animaux

Animal Training

That mutt (dog blog)	https://www.thatmutt.com/
Julie & Gary Stansbridge	57 route de Beaulieu 16460 Ventouse Tel: 05 45 68 91 25

Cadastral Plan

	http://www.cadastre.gouv.fr

Car Clean Air Sticker

	https://www.certificat-air.gouv.fr/en/demande

Dechetteries

	https://www.annuaire-mairie.fr/decheterie.html

DIY Stores, Building Supplies

Brico Depot	https://www.bricodepot.fr
Castorama	https://www.castorama.fr
Chausson	https://www.chausson-materiaux.fr/
Leroy Merlin	https://www.leroymerlin.fr
M Bricolage	https://www.mr-bricolage.fr

Useful Addresses

E-Agency

| PAP | https://www.pap.fr/ |

Expat News

| Connexion | https://www.connexionfrance.com/ |
| The Local | https://www.thelocal.fr/ |

Notaires

| Find by location | https://www.notaires.fr/en |

Nuisance/Cold Calls

| Bloctel | https://www.bloctel.gouv.fr/ |

Property Valuations

| By Area | https://app.dvf.etalab.gouv.fr/ |

Radio

France Info	https://www.francetvinfo.fr/en-direct/radio.html
France Inter	https://www.franceinter.fr/
Independent Radio Group	https://www.lesindesradios.fr/
Understand the world in French, (with Transcriptions)	https://savoirs.rfi.fr/fr/apprendre-enseigner/langue-française/journal-en-français-facile

Road Travel

| *Bison Fute* | https://www.bison-fute.gouv.fr/ |

Rugby

| Top 14 | https://www.lnr.fr/rugby-top-14 |
| Pro D2 | https://www.lnr.fr/rugby-pro-d2 |

Rugby Papers

| *L'Equipe* | https://www.lequipe.fr |
| Midi-Olympique | https://www.midi-olympique.fr |

Useful Addresses

Service-Public

Official administrative site for Frabnce	https://www.service-public.fr/

Sewage & Septic Tanks

SPANC	http://www.assainissement-non-collectif.developpement-durable.gouv.fr/le-service-public-d-assainissement-non-collectif-r11.html

Sport

Flashscore	https://www.flashscore.com/
Refereeing	https://www.tousarbitres.fr/

Supermarkets

Carrefour	https://www.carrefour.fr/
Casino	https://www.supercasino.fr/
Intermarche	https://www.intermarche.com/home.html
Leclerc	http://www.e-leclerc.com/
Lidl	https://www.lidl.fr/fr/index.htm
Monoprix	https://www.monoprix.fr
Super U	https://www.magasins-u.com/superu-lubersac

Tax Office

	http:www.impots.gouv.fr

Telephone Companies

Bouygues Telecom	https://www.bouyguestelecom.fr
Orange	https://www.orange.fr
SFR	https://www.sfr.fr

Television

Canal+	https://boutique.canal.fr/
Eurosport	http://www.eurosportplayer.fr
France 2	https://www.france.tv/france-2/

Useful Addresses

Utilities

For a comprehensive guide to setting up your utilities you would do worse than check out

https://en.selectra.info/guide-moving-to-france/utilities

Public Holidays 2019
Annex C

Date	French Name	Day of Week	Holiday
1 Jan	Jour de l'an	Tue	New Year's Day
19 Apr	Vendredi Saint	Fri	Good Friday *
22 Apr	Lundi de paques	Mon	Easter Monday
1 May	Fête du travail	Wed	Labour Day
8 May	Victoire	Wed	Victory Day
30 May	L'Ascension	Thu	Ascension Day
10 Jun	Lundi de Pentecôte	Mon	Whit Monday
14 Jul	Fête nationale	Sun	Bastille Day
15 Aug	L'Assomption	Thu	Assumption Day
1 Nov	La Toussaint	Fri	All Saints' Day
11 Nov	L'Armistice	Mon	Armistice Day
25 Dec	Noel	Wed	Christmas Day
26 Dec	Deuxième jour de Noel	Thu	St Stephen's Day *

* *Vendredi Saint* and *Deuxième jour de Noel* are observed in the Alsace and Moselle *départements* only

Public Holidays 2020
Annex D

Date	French Name	Day of Week	Holiday
1 Jan	Jour de l'an	Wed	New Year's Day
10 Apr	Vendredi Saint	Fri	Good Friday *
13 Apr	Lundi de paques	Mon	Easter Monday
1 May	Fête du travail	Fri	Labour Day
8 May	Victoire	Fri	Victory Day
21 May	L'Ascension	Thu	Ascension Day
1 Jun	Lundi de Pentecôte	Mon	Whit Monday
14 Jul	Fête nationale	Tue	Bastille Day
15 Aug	L'Assomption	Sat	Assumption Day
1 Nov	La Toussaint	Sun	All Saints' Day
11 Nov	L'Armistice	Wed	Armistice Day
25 Dec	Noel	Fri	Christmas Day
26 Dec	Deuxième jour de Noel	Sat	St Stephen's Day *

* *Vendredi Saint* and *Deuxième jour de Noel* are observed in the Alsace and Moselle *départements* only

13 June 2019